Shared
-PLATES-

THE AUSTRALIAN WOMEN'S WEEKLY
TRIPLE TESTED
TEST KITCHEN

THE AUSTRALIAN
Women's Weekly

- SHARED PLATES -

CONTENTS

the shared table 6

SMALL PLATES 8

LARGE PLATES 54

SIDE PLATES 112

SWEET PLATES 144

MENUS 178 GLOSSARY 182

CONVERSION CHART 187 INDEX 188

THE Shared TABLE

Eating has always been a communal activity. We gather around the dining table to share a meal with family, talking about school, work and everything else that has gone on throughout the day. We head out on the town for a special meal with friends, swapping stories of the highs and lows since the last get-together. We celebrate every milestone with food; after all, what would a birthday be without cake. Sharing a meal with those we love is universal – think of Christmas where various dishes are spread out on the table with everyone passing food around to serve themselves, surveying how much room they have left on their plate before adding another spoonful of mashed potato. This is the simple idea behind shared plates: everyone gets to try everything. They get to choose as much or as little as they like. It's like a buffet, but you don't have to get up from your chair.

Family-style service has traditionally differed from the experience of dining out where each person orders their own dish from the menu. They are served at the same time but, unless someone is feeling generous, everyone only gets to try their own meal. Lately, what was once the domain of home-cooked meals shared around the dining table has become trendy in restaurants. Inner city hotspots and suburban eateries alike have rushed to emulate the homemade charm of shared plates. They're all about bringing people together to sit and talk, drink, eat and enjoy each other's company.

At first glance, shared plates may seem like a casual approach; all you have to do is cook up a feast and then leave it to everyone else to serve themselves. But there's more to it than meets the eye. Like any meal, it's important to get a good mix of meat, vegies and salads. It also helps if you throw in some yummy starters. And it's vital there is a dessert or two to keep the crowd happy. All of these courses can be served in a variety of ways, but the most social is to pile them high on a shared plate so that everyone can get involved.

As much as shared plates are about the social experience, they're also an easy way to ensure that there's a balance of different dishes. Every good meal starts with a selection of appetisers, tapas or finger food. Whatever you want to call it, it's important these small plates can be consumed in one bite. Everyone should be able to balance a starter in one hand and a drink in the other, so ensure these tasty portions are just a tease for what's to come.

NEXT UP IS THE MAIN EVENT: LARGE PLATES THAT ARE LADEN WITH HEARTY, FILLING AND SUBSTANTIAL FOOD. OFTEN CENTRED ON MEAT OR SEAFOOD, THESE SHARED PLATES ARE MORE OF A SIT-DOWN AFFAIR. EMBRACE LARGER DISHES FOR A MORE RELAXED TAKE ON SHARING.

SIDE PLATES MAKE ANY MEAL SEEM EFFORTLESSLY PUT-TOGETHER. USE FRESH PRODUCE AND SEASONAL VEGIES TO CREATE LIGHT SALADS AND TEMPTING HOT SIDES.

AND WHAT MEAL WOULD BE COMPLETE WITHOUT A FEW TREATS? WHILE MANY PEOPLE HESITATE AT THE IDEA OF SHARING SWEET PLATES, IT CAN ACTUALLY BE A CONVENIENT EXCUSE FOR INDULGING IN MULTIPLE DESSERTS. WITH CAKES, TARTS, PUDDINGS, MERINGUES, BAKLAVA AND FRUIT SALAD ON OFFER, HOW COULD YOU CHOOSE JUST ONE?

There's an undeniable joy in sharing food with family and friends. Whether it's a quick weeknight meal or a lazy weekend catch-up, food is enriched by the company we share it with.

SMALL Plates

CHORIZO AND POTATO FRITTERS

PREP + COOK TIME 40 MINUTES MAKES 40

2 teaspoons vegetable oil

1 cured chorizo sausage (170g), chopped finely

1 small brown onion (80g), chopped finely

2 fresh small red thai (serrano) chillies, chopped finely

2 medium zucchini (240g), grated coarsely

450g (14½ ounces) bintje potatoes, grated coarsely

1 small kumara (orange sweet potato) (250g), grated coarsely

3 eggs, beaten lightly

1 cup (150g) plain (all-purpose) flour

1 teaspoon sweet paprika

vegetable oil, extra, for deep-frying

3 teaspoons sea salt flakes

¼ teaspoon paprika

½ cup (120g) sour cream

2 tablespoons sweet chilli sauce

½ cup loosely packed fresh coriander (cilantro) leaves

1 Heat oil in a medium frying pan; cook chorizo, onion and chilli, stirring, until onion softens. Add zucchini; cook, stirring, about 1 minute. Cool 10 minutes.

2 Combine chorizo mixture in a large bowl with potato, kumara, egg, flour and sweet paprika, season.

3 Fill a wok or large saucepan one-third full with extra oil; heat over medium heat to 180°C/350°F (or until a cube of bread turns golden in 10 seconds). Deep-fry level tablespoons of mixture, in batches, until fritters are browned lightly. Drain on paper towel.

4 Sprinkle fritters with combined salt and paprika. Serve with sour cream, sweet chilli sauce and coriander.

FISH SCROLLS WITH CAPSICUM SALSA

PREP + COOK TIME 40 MINUTES **MAKES** 30

You will need 30 small (15cm/6-inch) bamboo skewers and a large banana leaf (see tips).

1kg (2 pounds) firm white fish fillets

¼ cup (60ml) red wine vinegar

⅓ cup (80ml) olive oil

½ small red capsicum (bell pepper) (75g), chopped finely

½ small green capsicum (bell pepper) (75g), chopped finely

½ small red onion (50g), chopped finely

1 small tomato (90g), seeded, chopped finely

1 fresh long red chilli, seeded, sliced thinly

fresh coriander leaves (cilantro), to serve

1 Cut fish into 30 x 12cm (4¾-inch) strips, 1cm (½-inch) thick. Roll each strip into a scroll, secure with a skewer; season.

2 Combine vinegar and oil in a small saucepan; stir over low heat for 3 minutes or until warm – do not boil. Combine capsicum, onion and tomato in a small bowl; pour over warmed vinegar mixture, season to taste.

3 Meanwhile, heat an oiled large frying pan over medium-high heat; pan-fry fish, in batches, for 1½ minutes each side or until just cooked through.

4 Cut banana leaves into large rectangles; serve fish on banana leaves with capsicum salsa. Sprinkle over chilli and coriander.

tips Banana leaves can be ordered from fruit and vegetable stores. Cut with a sharp knife close to the main stem, then immerse in hot water so the leaves will be pliable. Depending on the shape of the fish, you may need to roll two pieces of fish together.

SMOKED OCEAN TROUT AND PICKLED FENNEL BUNS

PREP TIME 20 MINUTES (+ REFRIGERATION) MAKES 20

20 medium bread rolls (1kg), halved

1 cup (240g) spreadable cream cheese

2 baby cos (romaine) lettuces (360g), leaves separated

480g (15½ ounces) hot-smoked ocean trout or salmon fillets, flaked

4 small red radishes (140g), sliced thinly

1 small red onion (100g), sliced thinly into rings

PICKLED FENNEL

⅓ cup (80ml) strained lemon juice

2 tablespoons caster (superfine) sugar

2 tablespoons finely chopped fresh dill

1 tablespoon mustard seeds, toasted

1 tablespoon white wine vinegar

2 teaspoons sea salt flakes

4 baby fennel bulbs (520g), trimmed, sliced thinly

¼ cup (60ml) extra virgin olive oil

1 Make pickled fennel.
2 Spread bread roll bases with cream cheese; layer with lettuce, pickled fennel, trout, radish and onion. Top with bread roll lids.
3 Serve buns immediately on a large platter.

pickled fennel Whisk juice, sugar, dill, seeds, vinegar and salt until sugar dissolves. Add fennel, season to taste; toss to combine. Cover; refrigerate 30 minutes to allow flavours to develop. Drain and discard pickling liquid, then toss pickled fennel with olive oil.

tips Use a mandoline or V-slicer, available from kitchenware and department stores, to slice the fennel and radishes. For decoration and ease of handling either tie the rolls with kitchen string or secure them with toothpicks.

RICOTTA AND BASIL PANCAKES WITH ROASTED TOMATOES

PREP + COOK TIME 45 MINUTES MAKES 12

300g (9½ ounces) baby truss roma (egg) tomatoes

2 tablespoons extra virgin olive oil

1 cup (240g) ricotta

1 egg

1¼ cups (310ml) milk

1¼ cups (185g) self-raising flour

½ cup coarsely chopped fresh basil

¼ cup (20g) grated parmesan

30g (1 ounce) butter

1 tablespoon white balsamic vinegar

250g (8 ounces) rocket (arugula)

½ small red onion (50g), sliced thinly

1 Preheat oven to 220°C/425°F. Place tomatoes in a small baking dish; drizzle with half the oil. Season. Roast for 10 minutes or until skins just split.

2 Whisk ricotta and egg in a medium bowl until combined. Whisk in milk, then flour. Stir in basil and parmesan; season.

3 Melt a little of the butter in a large non-stick frying pan over medium heat. Pour ¼-cups of batter into pan, allowing room for spreading. Cook pancakes for 2 minutes each side or until golden and cooked through. Stack pancakes; cover to keep warm. Wipe out pan with paper towel; repeat with remaining butter and batter to make 12 pancakes in total.

4 Drizzle remaining oil and vinegar over rocket and onion in a medium bowl, season to taste; toss gently to combine.

5 Serve warm pancakes topped with rocket mixture, tomatoes and any remaining dressing.

WIPE THE PAN CLEAN WITH PAPER TOWEL BETWEEN

EACH BATCH OF PANCAKES SO THEY DON'T OVERBROWN.

MAKE YOUR OWN GUACAMOLE OR PICK SOME PREMADE UP FROM YOUR GREEN GROCER OR SUPERMARKET.

SHREDDED PORK CHIMICHANGA

PREP + COOK TIME 1 HOUR 50 MINUTES (+ COOLING) **SERVES** 16

500g (1 pound) diced pork

3 cloves garlic, peeled

2 black peppercorns

1 teaspoon ground cumin

3 cups (750ml) water

½ cup coarsely chopped fresh coriander (cilantro)

1 small red onion (80g), chopped finely

2 fresh green jalapeño chillies, seeded, chopped finely

8 x 20cm (8-inch) flour tortillas

vegetable oil, for deep-frying

1 Place pork, garlic, peppercorns, cumin and the water in a large saucepan; bring to the boil. Reduce heat; simmer, covered, for 1 hour or until pork is tender. Cool.

2 Drain liquid from pork; discard peppercorns and liquid. Shred pork and garlic using two forks. Combine pork mixture with coriander, onion and chilli in a large bowl; season.

3 Heat tortillas according to instructions on packet. Divide pork mixture evenly between tortillas. Roll tortillas up firmly, secure with toothpick at each end of roll.

4 Fill a wok or large frying pan one-third full with oil; heat over medium heat to 180°C/350°F (or until a cube of bread turns golden in 10 seconds). Deep-fry tortilla rolls, in batches, until browned lightly. Drain on paper towel. Remove toothpicks.

5 Cut each chimichanga in half; serve with guacamole, if you like.

HALOUMI AND AVOCADO BRUSCHETTA

PREP + COOK TIME 30 MINUTES **MAKES** 24

2 x 400g (12½-ounce) loaf afghan bread

cooking-oil spray

500g (1 pound) haloumi cheese

3 medium avocados (750g), mashed coarsely

1 medium red onion (170g), sliced thinly

400g (12½ ounces) cherry tomatoes, halved

1 tablespoon olive oil

2 tablespoons lemon juice

40g (1½ ounces) baby rocket leaves (arugula)

1 Preheat oven to 180°C/350°F. Line two oven trays with baking paper.

2 Roughly tear each loaf of bread into 12 pieces; spray both sides with cooking oil.

3 Place bread on oven trays; bake for 6 minutes or until browned lightly.

4 Cut haloumi into 24 thin slices; lay between 2 sheets of paper towel for 5 minutes.

5 Meanwhile, combine avocado, onion, tomato, oil and juice in a medium bowl. Season to taste.

6 Pan-fry haloumi, in batches, in an oiled large frying pan, for 1 minute each side or until browned.

7 Top bread with one slice of haloumi, some avocado mixture and a few rocket leaves to serve.

do-ahead Toast bread 2 hours ahead; store in an airtight container. Combine avocado mixture 1 hour ahead; store in the fridge. Haloumi is best cooked just before serving.

PAELLA CROQUETTES

PREP + COOK TIME 50 MINUTES (+ COOLING & REFRIGERATION) **MAKES** 12

1 cup (200g) white long-grain rice

2 cups (500ml) chicken stock

1 dried bay leaf

1 teaspoon ground turmeric

2 teaspoons olive oil

1 clove garlic, crushed

1 medium red onion (170g), chopped coarsely

1 cured chorizo sausage (170g), chopped coarsely

100g (3 ounces) smoked chicken, chopped coarsely

1 tablespoon finely chopped fresh flat-leaf parsley

¼ cup (35g) plain (all-purpose) flour

2 eggs, beaten lightly

1 tablespoon milk

1 cup (100g) packaged breadcrumbs

vegetable oil, for deep-frying

1 Combine rice, stock, bay leaf and turmeric in a medium saucepan; bring to the boil, stirring. Reduce heat; simmer, covered, for 12 minutes or until rice is tender. Remove from heat; stand, covered, 10 minutes. Fluff rice with fork, discard bay leaf; cool.

2 Meanwhile, heat olive oil in a large frying pan; cook garlic, onion and chorizo, stirring, until onion softens; cool.

3 Blend or process rice, chorizo mixture, chicken and parsley until ingredients come together; season to taste. With wet hands, shape ¼-cups of rice mixture into croquettes. Toss croquettes in flour; shake off excess. Dip in combined egg and milk, then in breadcrumbs. Place croquettes on baking-paper-lined tray; cover, refrigerate 30 minutes.

4 Fill a wok or large saucepan one-third full with vegetable oil; heat over medium heat to 180°C/350°F (or until a cube of bread turns golden in 10 seconds). Deep-fry croquettes, in batches, until browned lightly. Drain on paper towel.

PRIMAVERA SOUP WITH PANGRATTATO

PREP + COOK TIME 25 MINUTES **SERVES** 8

500g (1 pound) zucchini flowers, with zucchini attached

60g (2 ounces) butter

8 shallots (200g), chopped

2 litres (8 cups) vegetable stock

1 litre (4 cups) water

⅔ cup (150g) risoni pasta

300g (9½ ounces) asparagus, cut into 3cm (1¼-inch) lengths

4 cups (480g) frozen baby peas

2 teaspoons finely grated lemon rind

PANGRATTATO

400g (12½ ounces) crusty italian bread

⅓ cup (80ml) extra virgin olive oil

1 fresh long red chilli, chopped finely

4 cloves garlic, chopped

⅔ cup loosely packed small fresh flat-leaf parsley leaves

2 teaspoons finely grated lemon rind

1 Snap off flowers from zucchini; remove the yellow stamens from the centre of each flower. Cut zucchini in half lengthways.

2 Heat butter in a large saucepan over medium heat; cook shallots, stirring, for 3 minutes or until soft.

3 Add stock and the water to pan; bring to the boil. Add pasta and zucchini; simmer about 5 minutes, stirring occasionally.

4 Meanwhile, make pangrattato.

5 Add asparagus and peas to soup; simmer for 5 minutes or until just tender. Season to taste. Stir in zucchini flowers.

6 Ladle soup into bowls; top with pangrattato and rind.

pangrattato Remove crust from bread; tear bread into 1cm (½-inch) pieces. Heat oil in a large frying pan over medium-high heat; cook chilli and bread pieces, stirring, until browned lightly and crisp. Add garlic; cook until fragrant. Remove from heat; stir in parsley and rind. Season to taste.

PANGRATTATO IS THE ITALIAN NAME FOR BREADCRUMBS, WHICH CAN BE FINE OR COARSE. THESE ARE BEST MADE WITH DAY-OLD BREAD.

FRIED BUTTERMILK AND MUSTARD CHICKEN WINGS

PREP + COOK TIME 40 MINUTES (+ REFRIGERATION) SERVES 12

1 cup (300g) rock salt

1 cup (220g) firmly packed brown sugar

2 tablespoons finely grated lemon rind

2 tablespoons finely chopped fresh lemon thyme

1 clove garlic, crushed

1.5kg (3 pounds) chicken wing nibbles

¾ cup (105g) plain (all-purpose) flour, plus extra, to dust

600ml buttermilk

2 tablespoons hot english mustard

1 egg, beaten lightly

vegetable oil, for deep-frying

1 Place salt, sugar, rind, thyme and garlic in a large bowl; mix to combine. Add chicken, toss well to coat; cover, refrigerate 1 hour.

2 Wash salt mixture from chicken under cold water; pat chicken dry with paper towel.

3 Place flour in a large bowl; gradually whisk in combined buttermilk, mustard and egg. Season.

4 Fill a large saucepan or deep fryer one-third full with oil; heat over medium heat to 180°C/350°F (or until a cube of bread turns golden in 10 seconds). Dust chicken in extra flour then batter; drain excess batter. Deep-fry chicken, in batches, turning halfway, for 6 minutes or until golden and cooked through. Remove with a slotted spoon; drain on paper towel.

5 Serve chicken on a large platter with lemon salt (see tips), if you like.

tips Chicken wing nibbles are available from most major supermarkets. You could also use chicken drumettes. To make lemon salt, combine ½ cup sea salt flakes, the thinly sliced rind of 2 lemons and 2 tablespoons finely chopped fresh lemon thyme.

CHIPOTLE BEEF TOSTADITAS

PREP + COOK TIME 55 MINUTES (+ STANDING) MAKES 36

2 chipotle chillies

½ cup (125ml) boiling water

12 x 17cm (6¾-inch) round white corn tortillas

vegetable oil, for deep-frying

1 tablespoon vegetable oil, extra

1 small brown onion (80g), sliced thinly

1 clove garlic, crushed

280g (9 ounces) minced (ground) beef

1 tablespoon tomato paste

1 cup (250ml) beer

¼ cup coarsely chopped fresh coriander (cilantro)

½ cup (120g) sour cream

1 Cover chillies with the boiling water in a small heatproof bowl; stand 20 minutes.

2 Meanwhile, cut three 7cm (2¾-inch) rounds from each tortilla. Fill a wok or large saucepan one-third full with oil; heat over medium heat to 180°C/350°F (or until a cube of bread turns golden in 10 seconds). Deep-fry rounds, in batches, until browned lightly. Drain on paper towel.

3 Drain chillies over a small bowl; reserve liquid. Remove stems from chillies; discard stems. Blend or process chillies and reserved liquid until smooth.

4 Heat extra oil in a medium frying pan; cook onion, stirring, until softened. Add garlic and beef; cook, stirring, until beef is changed in colour. Stir in paste, beer and chilli puree; bring to the boil. Reduce heat; simmer, uncovered, for 15 minutes or until liquid is almost evaporated. Stir in coriander. Season to taste.

5 Top each tortilla crisp with a rounded teaspoon of chipotle beef then with ½ teaspoon of sour cream.

BEEF MIXTURE CAN BE MADE A DAY AHEAD;
STORE, COVERED, IN THE FRIDGE.
REHEAT BEFORE SERVING.

ARTICHOKE AND ASPARAGUS FRITTERS WITH OLIVE RELISH

PREP + COOK TIME 40 MINUTES MAKES 15

170g (5½ ounces) asparagus, trimmed, chopped finely

280g (9 ounces) bottled artichokes in brine, drained, chopped finely

2 eggs

2 tablespoons finely chopped fresh mint

½ cup (40g) finely grated parmesan

¼ cup (35g) self-raising flour

vegetable oil, for shallow-frying

OLIVE RELISH

½ cup (60g) seeded green olives, chopped finely

½ cup (60g) seeded black olives, chopped finely

¼ cup finely chopped fresh flat-leaf parsley

1 tablespoon finely chopped fresh chives

1 tablespoon olive oil

1 tablespoon lemon juice

1 Make olive relish.

2 Combine asparagus, artichoke, eggs, mint, parmesan and flour in a medium bowl, season.

3 Heat oil in a large frying pan; shallow-fry heaped tablespoons of fritter mixture, in batches, until browned all over and cooked through. Drain fritters on paper towel; serve hot with olive relish.

olive relish Combine ingredients in a small bowl.

tip Make relish a day ahead, cover, refrigerate.

ROAST PUMPKIN AND FETTA BRUSCHETTA

PREP + COOK TIME 50 MINUTES **MAKES** 30

1 long french bread stick (300g)

cooking-oil spray

1.5kg (3-pound) butternut pumpkin

1 teaspoon dried chilli flakes

1½ teaspoons cumin seeds

2 tablespoons extra virgin olive oil

½ cup (50g) walnuts, roasted, chopped coarsely

180g (5½ ounces) persian fetta, crumbled

1 tablespoon fresh thyme leaves

1 Preheat oven to 180°C/350°F. Line two oven trays with baking paper.

2 Trim rounded ends from bread. Cut bread into 30 x 1.5cm (¾-inch) thick slices; spray both sides with cooking oil. Place bread on oven trays. Bake for 8 minutes or until browned lightly. Cool on trays.

3 Meanwhile, cut pumpkin lengthways into four slices about 3cm (1¼-inch) thick. Cut each piece into 5mm (¼-inch) thick slices.

4 Place pumpkin, chilli, seeds and oil in a large bowl; toss well to combine. Arrange slices on two baking-paper-lined oven trays. Roast for 25 minutes or until just tender.

5 Top bread with 3-4 pumpkin slices; sprinkle over walnuts, fetta and thyme.

do-ahead Bread can be toasted 2 hours ahead; store in an airtight container. Pumpkin can be cooked 1 hour ahead.

CHIMICHURRI LAMB CUTLETS

PREP + COOK TIME 25 MINUTES (+ REFRIGERATION) **MAKES** 20

4 fresh long red chillies, seeded, chopped finely

3 cloves garlic, crushed

2 tablespoons red wine vinegar

2 teaspoons dried oregano

2 teaspoons ground cumin

2 teaspoons sweet paprika

1 large tomato (220g), chopped finely

1 large red onion (200g), chopped finely

½ cup firmly packed fresh flat-leaf parsley leaves, shredded finely

1 cup (250ml) extra virgin olive oil

20 frenched lamb cutlets (1kg)

1 To make chimichurri, place all ingredients except lamb in a large bowl, season; stir to combine.

2 Place half the chimichurri in a large bowl with lamb; toss to coat in marinade. Cover; refrigerate 3 hours or overnight. Cover remaining chimichurri; refrigerate until required.

3 Preheat a grill pan (or barbecue) over high heat. Cook lamb, turning occasionally, for 4 minutes for medium or until cooked to your liking. Cover lamb; rest for 5 minutes.

4 Place lamb cutlets on a large platter; serve with reserved chimichurri. Sprinkle over extra fresh parsley sprigs to serve, if you like.

tips If you are pressed for time, process all the chimichurri ingredients in a food processor until coarsely chopped. You can substitute chicken wings or drumsticks for the lamb cutlets, if you prefer.

FRIED OYSTERS WITH SALSA

PREP + COOK TIME 35 MINUTES MAKES 12

1 small tomato (90g), chopped finely

½ medium yellow capsicum (bell pepper) (100g), chopped finely

½ medium red onion (85g), chopped finely

1 tablespoon finely chopped fresh coriander (cilantro)

1 tablespoon olive oil

1 tablespoon lime juice

1 fresh small red thai (serrano) chilli, seeded, chopped finely

12 oysters on the half shell

½ cup (85g) polenta

⅓ cup (80ml) milk

1 egg, beaten lightly

pinch cayenne pepper

vegetable oil, for deep-frying

1 Preheat oven to 180°C/350°F.

2 Combine tomato, capsicum, onion, coriander, olive oil, juice and chilli in a small bowl; season to taste.

3 Remove oysters from shells; reserve oysters. Place shells on oven tray; heat in oven about 5 minutes.

4 Meanwhile, combine polenta, milk, egg and pepper in small bowl.

5 Fill a medium saucepan one-third full with vegetable oil; heat over medium heat to 180°C/350°F (or until a cube of bread turns golden in 10 seconds). Dip oysters in batter; deep-fry oysters, in batches, until browned lightly. Drain on paper towel. Return oysters to shells; top with salsa.

SOFT SHELL CRAB WITH GREEN ONION AÏOLI

PREP + COOK TIME 30 MINUTES SERVES 8

½ cup (100g) rice flour

1 teaspoon dried chilli flakes

2 teaspoons sea salt flakes

8 uncooked small soft shell crabs (500g)

vegetable oil, for deep-frying

1 cup loosely packed fresh basil leaves

GREEN ONION AÏOLI

¾ cup (225g) mayonnaise

2 green onions (scallions), sliced thinly

1 clove garlic, crushed

1 tablespoon lemon juice

1 Make green onion aïoli.

2 Combine flour, chilli and salt in a medium bowl.

3 Clean crabs; pat dry then cut into quarters. Coat crab with flour mixture; shake off excess.

4 Fill a wok or large saucepan one-third full with oil; heat over medium heat to 180°C/350°F (or until a cube of bread turns golden in 10 seconds). Deep-fry basil for 30 seconds or until crisp. Drain on paper towel. Deep-fry crab, in batches, until browned lightly. Drain on paper towel.

5 Serve crab with basil, aïoli and lemon wedges, if you like.

green onion aïoli Combine ingredients in a small bowl.

tip To clean the soft shell crabs, lift back the flap on undersides and wipe clean with a damp piece of paper towel. Never wash seafood under a running tap as this will wash away the 'sea' flavour and waterlog the seafood. If you need to rinse, hold the seafood in one hand over the sink and use your other hand to gently splash the seafood with as little water as possible.

INDIVIDUAL EGG, SPINACH AND TOMATO BREAD CASES

PREP + COOK TIME 40 MINUTES MAKES 8

cooking-oil spray

2 cob loaves (900g)

60g (2 ounces) baby spinach leaves

16 eggs

8 small heirloom tomatoes (240g), halved

200g (6½ ounces) ricotta

⅔ cup loosely packed fresh basil leaves

1 Preheat oven to 180°C/350°F. Spray eight 13cm (5¼-inch) individual pie tins with cooking oil. Place on an oven tray.

2 Cut eight 1.5cm (¾-inch) thick slices crossways from bread. Trim crusts from bread slices. Roll bread gently with rolling pin to flatten slightly. Line tins with bread slices; trim bread with kitchen scissors.

3 Bake bread cases for 10 minutes or until bread is dried out but not coloured.

4 Divide spinach leaves between bread cases; crack two eggs into each case, top with tomato. Drop small spoonfuls of ricotta into cases. Season.

5 Bake cases further 15 minutes or until the egg whites are set. Sprinkle with basil.

tips You can use halved cherry, grape or mini roma (egg) tomatoes if you like. This recipe would make a delicious breakfast or brunch dish.

serving suggestion Green salad or steamed asparagus.

RECIPE CAN BE PREPARED A DAY AHEAD
UP TO THE END OF STEP 3; STORE,
COVERED, IN THE FRIDGE.

FIVE SPICE SQUID WITH LIME MAYONNAISE

PREP + COOK TIME 40 MINUTES **SERVES** 24

2 tablespoons chinese five-spice

1 tablespoon ground ginger

1 teaspoon sea salt flakes, crushed

3 teaspoons onion powder

2 tablespoons self-raising flour

½ cup (75g) cornflour (cornstarch)

600g (1¼ pounds) cleaned small squid (hoods and tentacles)

vegetable oil, for deep-frying

4 green onions (scallions), sliced thinly diagonally

2 fresh long red chillies, sliced thinly diagonally

4 limes, each cut into 6 wedges

LIME MAYONNAISE

2 teaspoons finely grated lime rind

2 teaspoons lime juice

2 cups (600g) japanese mayonnaise

1 Make lime mayonnaise.

2 Combine spices, salt and onion powder in a large bowl; reserve one-third of spice mixture. Add flours to remaining mixture; stir to combine.

3 Cut each squid hood in half lengthways. Score inside in a criss-cross pattern with a sharp knife, then cut into 1.5cm (½-inch) wide strips.

4 Fill a large wok one-third full with oil; heat to 180°C/350°F (or until a cube of bread turns golden in 10 seconds). Toss squid and tentacles in flour spice mix; shake away excess. Fry squid, in batches, for 2 minutes or until golden and just tender; drain on paper towel. Transfer to a large bowl.

5 Fry onion and chilli for 2 minutes or until golden. Using a slotted spoon, remove from oil, add to bowl with squid; toss well to combine.

6 Divide squid into ¼-cup serving cones. Sprinkle with reserved spice mix to serve; accompany with lime mayonnaise and lime wedges.

lime mayonnaise Combine ingredients in a small bowl. Cover, refrigerate until ready to serve.

tips To clean squid, gently pull head and tentacles with internal sac away from body. Remove clear cartilage (quill) from inside body. Cut tentacles from head just below the eyes; discard head. Remove and discard side fins and skin from body with salted fingers. Wash the body and tentacles thoroughly; pat dry. Japanese mayonnaise, from Asian grocers and selected supermarkets, is made with rice vinegar and has a slightly different taste from regular mayonnaise, which may be substituted.

BAKED RICOTTA WITH CHAR-GRILLED VEGETABLES

PREP + COOK TIME 1 HOUR 15 MINUTES MAKES 12

cooking-oil spray

750g (1½ pounds) firm ricotta

1 egg

¼ cup (20g) finely grated parmesan

¼ cup chopped fresh chives

¼ teaspoon dried chilli flakes

5 fresh bay leaves

1 medium eggplant (440g), cut lengthways into 5mm (¼-inch) slices

2 medium red capsicums (bell peppers) (400g), cut into eight thick slices

2 medium zucchini (240g), sliced thinly lengthways

12 slices wholegrain sourdough bread (135g)

SALSA VERDE

1¾ cups loosely packed fresh basil leaves

2 cups loosely packed fresh flat-leaf parsley leaves

2 cloves garlic, crushed

2 anchovy fillets, chopped

2 teaspoons rinsed, drained baby capers

1 teaspoon finely grated lemon rind

⅓ cup (80ml) extra virgin olive oil

2 teaspoons lemon juice

1 Preheat oven to 180°C/350°F. Spray an 18cm (7¼-inch) springform pan with cooking oil; line base and side with baking paper.

2 Combine ricotta, egg, parmesan and chives in a large bowl; season. Spoon mixture into pan, level surface and sprinkle with chilli flakes. Bake for 35 minutes or until puffed and centre is firm. Stand in pan for 5 minutes before transferring to a platter. Press bay leaves on top.

3 Meanwhile, make salsa verde.

4 Spray vegetables and bread slices with cooking oil; season. Cook vegetables on a grill plate (or grill or barbecue) over medium-high heat for 2 minutes each side or until charred and tender. Char-grill bread for 1 minute each side or until lightly charred.

5 Serve baked ricotta with vegetables, bread and salsa verde.

salsa verde Process herbs, garlic, anchovy, capers, rind and half the oil until coarsely chopped. With motor operating, add remaining oil in a thin stream, processing until mixture is smooth. Transfer mixture to a small bowl, stir in juice; season to taste. Cover surface with plastic wrap.

ZUCCHINI TARTS

PREP + COOK TIME 40 MINUTES **SERVES** 8

2 sheets puff pastry

½ cup (125g) mascarpone cheese

2 eggs

½ cup (40g) grated parmesan

340g (11 ounces) baby zucchini, sliced thinly lengthways

1 Preheat oven to 220°C/425°F. Line two oven trays with baking paper.

2 Cut pastry sheets in half; place two halves on each tray about 5cm (2 inches) apart. With the back of a small knife, mark a 1cm (½-inch) border on pastry pieces. Prick bases inside border with a fork.

3 Bake pastry for 10 minutes or until golden. Using a clean tea towel, press down carefully on the centre of each tart.

4 Meanwhile, combine mascarpone, eggs and 1 tablespoon of the parmesan in a medium bowl; season well.

5 Spread egg mixture over tart bases; top with zucchini slices, slightly overlapping. Sprinkle with remaining parmesan.

6 Bake tarts for 12 minutes or until golden.

tip Use a mandoline or V-slicer to slice the zucchini quickly and evenly.

serving suggestion Tomato and basil salad.

RATATOUILLE SOUP WITH PISTOU

PREP + COOK TIME 45 MINUTES SERVES 6

2 tablespoons extra virgin olive oil

2 medium red onions (340g), chopped coarsely

1 medium eggplant (300g), chopped coarsely

2 medium red capsicums (bell peppers) (400g), chopped coarsely

4 cloves garlic, chopped coarsely

2 medium green zucchini (240g), chopped coarsely

800g (1½ pounds) canned diced tomatoes

1 litre (4 cups) vegetable stock

2 x 110g (3½-ounce) mini baguettes

300g (9½ ounces) ricotta

½ cup (40g) finely grated parmesan

PISTOU

2 cloves garlic, peeled

¼ cup (60ml) extra virgin olive oil

1 cup loosely packed fresh basil leaves

1 Heat oil in a large saucepan over medium heat; cook onion, stirring, for 5 minutes or until soft. Add eggplant, capsicum and garlic; cook, covered, over low heat, for 20 minutes or until soft.

2 Add zucchini, tomatoes and stock; simmer, covered, for 10 minutes or until zucchini is tender. Season to taste.

3 Meanwhile, make pistou.

4 Preheat grill (broiler).

5 Split bread lengthways, then in half crossways. Spread with 2 tablespoons of the pistou then ricotta; sprinkle with parmesan. Place on an oven tray under the grill until browned lightly.

6 Ladle soup into serving bowls; top with remaining pistou. Serve with bread.

pistou Blend or process ingredients until almost smooth. Season to taste. Transfer to a small bowl; cover tightly with plastic wrap.

tip This soup is not suitable to freeze.

PRAWN PAD THAI

PREP + COOK TIME 1 HOUR (+ STANDING) **SERVES** 12

2 tablespoons small dried shrimp

400g (12½ ounces) dried rice noodles

⅓ cup (80ml) peanut or vegetable oil

¼ cup (60ml) boiling water

½ cup (135g) grated palm sugar

1 tablespoon tamarind puree (concentrate)

¼ cup (60ml) lime juice

⅓ cup (80ml) fish sauce

2 tablespoons soy sauce

800g (1½ pounds) uncooked medium king prawns (shrimp)

⅔ cup (100g) roasted unsalted peanuts

3 cloves garlic, crushed

1 fresh long red chilli, chopped finely

3 eggs, beaten lightly

6 green onions (scallions), sliced thinly diagonally

½ cup (40g) fried asian shallots

150g (4½ ounces) bean sprouts

1 cup firmly packed coriander leaves (cilantro)

2 limes, each cut into 6 wedges

1 Place shrimp in a small heatproof bowl, cover with boiling water; stand 30 minutes or until softened. Drain; chop finely. Place noodles in a large heatproof bowl; cover with boiling water. Stand 15 minutes or until just tender. Drain noodles, toss with 2 teaspoons of the oil; cover with plastic wrap to prevent drying out.

2 Stir the boiling water, sugar, tamarind, juice and sauces in a small jug or bowl until sugar dissolves.

3 Shell and devein prawns, leaving tails intact. Chop half the nuts coarsely; chop remaining nuts finely.

4 Heat a wok over high heat; add 1 tablespoon of the oil. Add prawns; stir-fry for 2 minutes or until just beginning to change colour; remove from wok.

5 Add remaining oil, shrimp, garlic and chilli to wok; stir-fry for 1 minute or until garlic is fragrant. Add egg; stir-fry for 1 minute or until just set. Add noodles, prawns, three-quarters of the green onion and sauce mixture; stir-fry until noodles are heated through.

6 Remove from heat; sprinkle over finely chopped peanuts and half the shallots; toss to combine.

7 Divide pad thai between 12 x 1-cup containers or boxes. Combine coarsely chopped peanuts, bean sprouts, remaining green onion and shallots, and coriander in a medium bowl; sprinkle over pad thai; serve with wedges.

tip Recipe can be prepared 4 hours ahead up to the end of step 4.

MIDDLE-EASTERN SALAD CUPS

PREP + COOK TIME 40 MINUTES (+ COOLING) MAKES 28

You will need 3 x 12-hole (2-tablespoon/40ml) deep flat-based patty pans; if you only have one pan, make the cups in batches. You also need an 8cm (3¼-inch) round cutter.

1 large potato (300g), unpeeled

2 x 26cm (10½-inch) round pitta breads

¼ cup (60ml) olive oil

2 medium lebanese cucumbers (340g)

2 large tomatoes (440g), seeded, chopped finely

½ small red onion (50g), chopped finely

2 small red radishes (70g), trimmed, sliced thinly

SUMAC DRESSING

1 clove garlic, crushed

1 teaspoon sumac

1 teaspoon sea salt flakes

¼ cup (60ml) lemon juice

¼ cup (60ml) olive oil

1 Preheat oven to 200°C/400°F. Oil 3 x 12-hole (2-tablespoon/40ml) deep flat-based patty pans.

2 Boil, steam or microwave potato until just tender. When cool enough to handle, peel, chop finely; cool.

3 Meanwhile, using an 8cm round cutter, cut out seven bread rounds; separate rounds into two layers. Repeat with remaining bread; you will have 28 bread rounds. Brush inside (rough side) of each round with a little of the oil.

4 Firmly push bread rounds, oiled-side up, into pan holes. Bake for 5 minutes or until golden; cool.

5 Meanwhile, make sumac dressing.

6 Seed and finely chop one cucumber. Combine potato, chopped cucumber, tomato and onion in a medium bowl. Add dressing, stir gently to combine.

7 To serve, using a vegetable peeler, cut remaining cucumber into thin slices; place into each bread cup with a few slices of radish. Spoon 1 tablespoon salad into each bread cup; sprinkle with extra sumac and top with a parsley sprig and fresh mint leaves, if you like.

sumac dressing Combine ingredients in a small screw-top jar; shake well to combine.

do-ahead Bread cups can be made a day ahead; store in an airtight container.

tip Buy fresh, thin-style pitta bread; if the bread is too thick it may not fit into the patty pan.

LARGE
Plates

CHAR-GRILLED QUAIL WITH CAULIFLOWER SALAD

PREP + COOK TIME 1 HOUR SERVES 8

1 large cauliflower (2kg), cut into 1.5cm (¾-inch) florets

¼ cup (60ml) olive oil

12 medium quails (2kg), butterflied (see tips)

1 tablespoon ground coriander

2 teaspoons ground cinnamon

2 tablespoons fresh thyme leaves

⅓ cup (80ml) pomegranate molasses

4 lebanese cucumbers (520g), diced

2 medium red onions (340g), chopped finely

8 green onions (scallions), sliced thinly

2⅔ cups chopped fresh flat-leaf parsley

1 cup chopped fresh mint

2 medium pomegranates (640g), seeds removed

½ cup (125ml) lemon juice

½ cup (125ml) extra virgin olive oil

1 teaspoon honey

1 Preheat oven to 220°C/425°F.

2 Divide cauliflower between two large oven trays; drizzle each tray with 2 teaspoons of the olive oil. Season. Bake for 15 minutes or until browned well.

3 Place quails on two large oven trays, sprinkle with spices, drizzle with remaining olive oil; season. Cook quails, skin-side down first, on a heated grill plate (or barbecue) over medium-high heat, for 3 minutes each side or until browned. Return quails to tray; top with thyme, drizzle with half the molasses. Bake for 8 minutes or until just cooked. Cover quail with foil; rest for 5 minutes.

4 Meanwhile, place cauliflower in a large bowl with cucumber, onions, herbs and half the pomegranate seeds. Whisk juice, extra virgin olive oil and honey in a small bowl. Pour dressing over salad; toss gently to combine.

5 Cut quails in half. Serve quail with cauliflower salad, drizzled with pan juices and remaining pomegranate molasses. Sprinkle with remaining pomegranate seeds.

tips To butterfly quails, cut down either side of the backbone with kitchen scissors, poultry shears or a knife; discard backbone, open quails out flat. To remove seeds from a pomegranate, cut a whole pomegranate in half and scrape the seeds from flesh with your fingers while holding the pomegranate upside down in a bowl of cold water; the seeds will sink and the white pith will float.

WARM BEEF SALAD WITH CHIMICHURRI

PREP + COOK TIME 1 HOUR 5 MINUTES (+ STANDING) SERVES 8

You will need to start this recipe the day before as the black-eyed peas must be soaked overnight.

2 cups (400g) black-eyed peas

6 medium corn cobs (2.4kg), husks removed

¼ cup (60ml) olive oil

6 x 200g (6½-ounce) sirloin steaks, trimmed

1 tablespoon each ground cumin and smoked paprika

2 medium red onions (340g), halved, sliced thinly

500g (1 pound) heirloom tomatoes, halved

2 medium avocados (500g), chopped

3 fresh long red chillies, sliced thinly

1 cup fresh coriander (cilantro) leaves

⅓ cup (80ml) lime juice

⅓ cup (80ml) extra virgin olive oil

CHIMICHURRI

4 cloves garlic, crushed

2 cups coarsely chopped fresh flat-leaf parsley leaves

1 cup coarsely chopped fresh coriander (cilantro) leaves

2 teaspoons ground cumin

2 fresh small red thai (serrano) chillies, chopped finely

1 cup (250ml) extra virgin olive oil

1½ tablespoons lime juice

1 Place black-eyed peas in a medium bowl of cold water; soak overnight.

2 Drain black-eyed peas. Cook peas in a large saucepan of boiling water for 15 minutes or until tender; drain. Rinse under cold water; drain well.

3 Meanwhile, make chimichurri.

4 Brush corn with a little of the oil; season. Cook corn on a heated grill plate (or barbecue) over medium heat, turning occasionally, for 15 minutes or until charred and tender. Cool 10 minutes. Cut kernels from cobs.

5 Brush steaks with a little of the oil, sprinkle with cumin and paprika; season. Cook steaks on heated grill plate over medium-high heat, for 3 minutes each side, depending on thickness, for medium rare or until cooked as desired. Remove from pan; cover with foil, rest 5 minutes.

6 Place peas and corn kernels in a large bowl with onion, tomato, avocado, chilli, coriander, juice, extra virgin olive oil and a third of the chimichurri, season; toss gently to combine.

7 Serve salad topped with sliced steak and drizzled with remaining chimichurri.

chimichurri Process garlic, herbs, cumin, chilli and 1 tablespoon of the oil until roughly chopped. With motor operating, add remaining oil in a thin steady stream until smooth. Stir in juice. Season to taste.

CHIMICHURRI IS A TRADITIONAL ARGENTINIAN HERB SAUCE SERVED WITH GRILLED MEATS.

KAFFIR LIME LEAVES ARE SOLD FRESH,
DRIED OR FROZEN. A STRIP OF LIME PEEL
MAY BE USED AS A SUBSTITUTE.

LIME LEAF CHICKEN

PREP + COOK TIME 45 MINUTES (+ REFRIGERATION) **SERVES** 8

12 kaffir lime leaves, chopped

4 cloves garlic, chopped

1 fresh long red chilli, chopped coarsely

¼ cup (50g) coarsely chopped fresh galangal

2 x 10cm (4-inch) sticks fresh lemon grass (20g), chopped coarsely

1 small red onion (100g), chopped coarsely

½ teaspoon chinese five-spice

1 teaspoon brown sugar

½ teaspoon freshly ground black pepper

2 tablespoons fish sauce

2 tablespoons vegetable oil

8 chicken maryland pieces (2.8kg)

¼ cup (60ml) extra virgin olive oil

400g (12½ ounces) dried thai rice noodles

2 cups (160g) bean sprouts

1 cup loosely packed fresh mint leaves

1 cup loosely packed fresh coriander (cilantro) leaves

2 medium limes (180g), cut into wedges

1 Place lime leaves, garlic, chilli, galangal, lemon grass and onion in a food processor or mortar. Add five spice, sugar, pepper, sauce and vegetable oil; process, or pound with a pestle, to form a thick paste.

2 Rub paste all over chicken pieces in a shallow dish. Cover; refrigerate 4 hours or overnight.

3 Preheat oven to 200°C/400°F.

4 Place chicken in a single layer on a baking-paper-lined oven tray; drizzle with olive oil. Roast for 30 minutes or until chicken is cooked through.

5 Meanwhile, place noodles in a large heatproof bowl; cover with hot water. Stand 20 minutes; drain. Rinse under cold water; drain well. Place noodles in a large bowl with sprouts and herbs; toss to combine.

6 Serve chicken with salad and lime wedges.

tips Galangal is related to ginger but is more dense in texture. Wash and scrape any woody parts before chopping or pounding to use. Chicken marylands are the joined thigh and drumstick. If unavailable, use thighs and drumsticks.

TOMATO BRAISED LAMB SHANKS WITH CREAMY POLENTA

PREP + COOK TIME 4 HOURS **SERVES** 8

2 tablespoons olive oil

16 french-trimmed lamb shanks (4kg)

1 large red onion (300g), sliced thinly

1 clove garlic, crushed

2 tablespoons tomato paste

1 cup (250ml) dry red wine

2 cups (500ml) chicken stock

1 cup (250ml) water

400g (12½ ounces) canned diced tomatoes

2 tablespoons coarsely chopped fresh rosemary

CREAMY POLENTA

3 cups (750ml) water

2 cups (500ml) milk

1 cup (250ml) chicken stock

1½ cups (250g) polenta

½ cup (40g) coarsely grated parmesan

1 cup (250ml) pouring cream

1 Preheat oven to 200°C/400°F.

2 Heat half the oil in a large flameproof baking dish; cook lamb, in batches, until browned. Remove from dish.

3 Heat remaining oil in same dish; cook onion and garlic, stirring, until onion softens. Add paste; cook, stirring, about 2 minutes. Add wine; bring to the boil. Boil, uncovered, until reduced by half.

4 Return lamb to dish with stock, the water, undrained tomatoes and rosemary. Cover; bake for 3 hours or until lamb is tender.

5 Remove lamb from dish; cover to keep warm. Reserve pan juices.

6 Meanwhile, make creamy polenta.

7 Divide polenta among serving plates; top with lamb shanks and reserved pan juices.

creamy polenta Bring the water, milk and stock to the boil in a medium saucepan; gradually stir in polenta. Cook, stirring, for 10 minutes or until polenta thickens slightly. Stir in parmesan and cream. Season with salt and pepper.

ROAST CHICKEN WITH BROAD BEANS AND LEMON

PREP + COOK TIME 1 HOUR 15 MINUTES SERVES 8

2 medium lemons (280g)

6 cups (750g) fresh shelled broad (fava) beans

¼ cup (60ml) olive oil

3kg (6 pounds) chicken pieces, bone-in, skin-on

6 green onions (scallions), cut into 4cm (1½-inch) lengths

6 cloves garlic, sliced thinly

12 sprigs fresh thyme

2¼ cups (560ml) chicken stock

¾ cup loosely packed fresh mint leaves

2 tablespoons rinsed, drained capers

1 Preheat oven to 200°C/400°F.

2 Using a vegetable peeler, peel eight 7cm (2¾-inch) strips of rind from lemons. Squeeze juice from lemons; you will need ¼ cup (60ml) juice.

3 Cook broad beans in a saucepan of boiling water about 2 minutes; drain. Refresh under cold running water; drain. Peel away skins then discard.

4 Heat oil in a large casserole dish over high heat; cook chicken pieces, in batches, for 3 minutes each side or until browned. Remove from dish; drain excess fat from dish.

5 Add onion, garlic, thyme and rind strips to same dish; cook about 2 minutes. Return chicken and any juices to the dish with stock; bring to the boil. Transfer to the oven; cook, uncovered, for 40 minutes or until chicken is cooked through. Stir in broad beans; cook a further 5 minutes or until heated through.

6 Serve chicken drizzled with lemon juice, topped with mint and capers.

tips You will need to buy about 3.2kg (6¼ pounds) fresh broad beans in the pod to yield 6 cups, or you can use frozen broad beans. You can cook baby potatoes with the chicken. If you prefer, you can use 2 x 1.5kg (3-pound) whole chickens chopped into pieces.

serving suggestion Serve with wholemeal couscous.

BARBECUED LAMB LEG WITH LEMON THYME SALSA VERDE

PREP + COOK TIME 1 HOUR SERVES 8

1.6kg (3¼ pounds) kumara (orange sweet potato), cut into thick wedges

¼ cup (60ml) olive oil

2 teaspoons chilli flakes

4 cloves garlic, crushed

2 tablespoons finely grated lemon rind

¼ cup (60ml) olive oil, extra

2 x 800g (1½-pound) butterflied lamb legs

LEMON THYME SALSA VERDE

4 cups loosely packed fresh flat-leaf parsley

¼ cup loosely packed fresh lemon thyme

2 tablespoons drained capers

2 cloves garlic, crushed

2 teaspoons caster (superfine) sugar

1 cup (250ml) olive oil

¼ cup (60ml) white wine vinegar

1 Preheat oven to 220°C/425°F.

2 Combine kumara, oil and chilli on a baking-paper-lined oven tray until well coated; season. Roast kumara for 40 minutes or until browned and cooked through.

3 Meanwhile, combine garlic, rind and extra oil in a large bowl; season. Add lamb; rub oil mixture all over lamb. Cook lamb on a heated grill plate (or grill or barbecue) over medium heat for 15 minutes each side for medium or until cooked as desired. Adjust the temperature if cooking too quickly or too slowly. Transfer to a tray; cover with foil, stand 10 minutes.

4 Meanwhile, make lemon thyme salsa verde.

5 Serve lamb sliced with kumara wedges and salsa verde.

lemon thyme salsa verde Blend or process ingredients until well combined. Season to taste.

tips You can ask the butcher to butterfly the lamb for you. Salsa verde can be made 6 hours ahead; cover surface with plastic wrap then cover tightly to prevent discolouring. Refrigerate until ready to use.

YOU WILL NEED ABOUT 6 LIMES FOR THIS RECIPE. NAM JIM CAN BE MADE A DAY AHEAD; KEEP TIGHTLY COVERED IN THE FRIDGE UNTIL READY TO USE.

STEAK WITH CASHEW NAM JIM AND ASIAN GREENS

PREP + COOK TIME 40 MINUTES SERVES 8

1.6kg (3¼ pounds) thick-cut rump steak

2 tablespoons peanut oil

700g (1½ pounds) gai lan

540g (1 pound) baby buk choy, trimmed, quartered

200g (6½ ounces) snow peas

8 green onions (scallions), sliced thinly

½ cup (80g) unsalted roasted cashews, chopped coarsely

½ cup loosely packed fresh coriander (cilantro) sprigs

CASHEW NAM JIM

4 shallots (100g), chopped

4 cloves garlic

4 fresh long green chillies, seeded, chopped

4 fresh coriander (cilantro) roots, chopped

5cm (2-inch) piece fresh ginger (20g), chopped

⅓ cup (90) grated dark palm sugar

⅔ cup (100g) unsalted roasted cashews

⅔ cup (160ml) lime juice, approximately

2 tablespoons fish sauce, approximately

1 Make cashew nam jim.

2 Trim fat from steak; rub with oil, season. Cook steak on a heated grill plate (or grill or barbecue) on medium-high heat for 4 minutes each side for medium or until cooked as desired. Remove steak from heat; cover with foil, rest 5 minutes.

3 Meanwhile, trim gai lan stalks; cut stalks from leaves. Steam stalks, in a single layer, in a large steamer over a wok or large saucepan of boiling water about 1 minute. Place separated buk choy on top; steam a further 2 minutes. Add snow peas and gai lan leaves; steam a further 2 minutes or until vegetables are just tender.

4 Place vegetables on a platter in layers, top with thickly sliced steak, and drizzle with any meat juices; top with cashew nam jim. Sprinkle with onion, nuts and coriander.

cashew nam jim Blend shallots, garlic, chilli, coriander root, ginger, sugar and nuts until mixture forms a paste. Transfer to a small bowl; stir in juice and sauce to taste.

serving suggestion Serve with steamed jasmine or brown rice.

BEEF FILLET WITH GARLIC CREAM SAUCE

PREP + COOK TIME 1 HOUR 20 MINUTES **SERVES** 8

1.5kg (3 pounds) baby beetroot (beets), trimmed

1kg (2 pounds) baby new potatoes

8 cloves garlic, unpeeled

⅓ cup (80ml) olive oil

1.5kg (3-pound) piece centre-cut beef eye fillet

2 tablespoons fresh rosemary leaves

1 tablespoon fresh thyme leaves

500g (1 pound) baby spinach leaves

GARLIC CREAM SAUCE

1 tablespoon olive oil

2 shallots (50g), chopped finely

½ cup (125ml) dry white wine

1 tablespoon plain (all-purpose) flour

300ml pouring cream

2 teaspoons dijon mustard

2 tablespoons lemon juice

2 tablespoons finely chopped fresh flat-leaf parsley

1 Preheat oven to 200°C/400°F. Line two shallow medium baking dishes with baking paper.

2 Scrub beetroot; place in one dish. Place potatoes and garlic in second dish. Drizzle beetroot and potatoes with 1 tablespoon of oil each; toss to coat. Roast about 20 minutes.

3 Meanwhile, tie kitchen string around beef at 3cm (1¼-inch) intervals. Heat 1 tablespoon of the remaining oil in a large frying pan over high heat; cook beef, turning, until browned all over. Season; scatter with herbs.

4 Separate garlic from potatoes. Place beef on potatoes; return to oven, cook with vegetables for a further 30 minutes or until beef is done as desired. Transfer beef to a tray; cover, stand 10 minutes. Cover vegetables to keep warm.

5 Squeeze garlic from skins; discard skins. Reserve garlic for sauce.

6 Make garlic cream sauce.

7 Heat remaining oil in a wok or large frying pan over high heat; cook spinach for 1 minute or until wilted. Season to taste.

8 Serve slices of beef with potatoes, beetroot, spinach and sauce.

garlic cream sauce Heat oil in a medium saucepan over medium-high heat; cook shallots, stirring, until soft. Add wine; bring to the boil. Boil, uncovered, for 3 minutes or until reduced by half. Add flour; cook, stirring, until mixture thickens and bubbles. Gradually stir in garlic puree, cream and mustard; stir until mixture boils and thickens. Stir in juice and parsley; season to taste.

tips You can use 1 small brown onion instead of the shallots, if you prefer. This recipe is best made close to serving.

YOU CAN USE SCOTCH FILLET INSTEAD OF EYE FILLET BUT ALLOW LONGER COOKING TIME AS THE PIECE IS THICKER.

ROAST VEAL RACK WITH CELERIAC AND POTATO GRATIN

PREP + COOK TIME 1 HOUR 50 MINUTES **SERVES** 8

2kg (4-pound) veal rack (8 cutlets)

1 cup (250ml) water

¼ cup (70g) dijon mustard

2 tablespoons horseradish cream

2 cloves garlic, crushed

1½ tablespoons plain (all-purpose) flour

2 teaspoons wholegrain mustard

2 cups (500ml) beef stock

2 tablespoons finely chopped fresh tarragon

1 tablespoon coarsely chopped fresh thyme

¼ cup finely chopped fresh flat-leaf parsley

CELERIAC AND POTATO GRATIN

600ml thickened (heavy) cream

3 cloves garlic, sliced thinly

3 teaspoons coarsely chopped fresh thyme leaves

1 medium celeriac (celery root) (750g), trimmed

3 medium potatoes (600g)

50g (1½ ounces) smoked cheddar, grated coarsely

1 teaspoon fresh thyme, extra

1 Preheat oven to 180°C/350°F.

2 Make celeriac and potato gratin.

3 Meanwhile, place veal on a wire rack in a flameproof roasting pan; pour the water into the base of the pan. Combine dijon mustard, horseradish and garlic in a small bowl. Spread mustard mixture over veal; season. Roast veal for last 45 minutes of gratin cooking time or until cooked as desired. Transfer veal to a plate. Cover; rest 10 minutes.

4 Heat roasting pan over medium-high heat, add flour; cook, whisking, until mixture is smooth and bubbly. Add wholegrain mustard and stock; stir until mixture boils and thickens. Season to taste.

5 Combine herbs; press onto veal. Cut veal into cutlets; serve with gratin and mustard sauce.

celeriac and potato gratin Place cream, garlic and thyme in a medium saucepan over medium heat; bring to a simmer. Remove from heat; stand 10 minutes. Meanwhile, using a mandoline or V-slicer, thinly slice celeriac and potatoes; combine in a large bowl. Layer celeriac and potato with cream mixture and salt and pepper in a 1.5-litre (6-cup) round ovenproof dish. Sprinkle with cheese. Cover with foil; bake about 1 hour. Uncover, bake for 20 minutes or until tender and golden. Top with extra thyme.

serving suggestion Serve with roman or green beans.

SLOW-COOKER RED PORK CURRY

PREP + COOK TIME 4 HOURS 45 MINUTES SERVES 8

1⅔ cups (400ml) coconut milk

1 cup (250ml) salt-reduced chicken stock

¼ cup (75g) thai red curry paste

2 tablespoons fish sauce

3 kaffir lime leaves, shredded finely

1.5kg (3 pounds) rindless boneless pork belly, cut into 3cm (1¼-inch) pieces

2 large kumara (orange sweet potatoes) (1kg), chopped coarsely

270g (8½ ounces) snake beans, chopped coarsely

1 cup loosely packed fresh thai basil leaves

2 fresh long red chillies, sliced thinly

1 kaffir lime leaf, shredded finely, extra

1 Combine coconut milk, stock, curry paste, sauce and lime leaves in a 4.5-litre (18-cup) slow cooker. Add pork and kumara; cook, covered, on high, for 4½ hours or until pork is tender.

2 Skim fat from surface; discard. Place beans on surface of curry; cook a further 5 minutes. Season to taste.

3 Serve curry sprinkled with basil, chilli and extra lime leaf.

tips Ask the butcher to chop the pork belly for you. If you have the time, refrigerate the curry at the end of step 1 until cold; this will solidify the fat and make it easy to remove. This recipe is suitable to freeze at the end of step 2.

serving suggestion Serve with steamed jasmine rice.

BAO ARE STEAMED CHINESE BUNS, ADAPTED BY MIGRANTS IN MANY OTHER ASIAN COUNTRIES.

SPICED TOFU BAO

PREP + COOK TIME 1 HOUR MAKES 8

375g (12 ounces) firm tofu

2 teaspoons chinese five-spice

1 teaspoon chilli powder

2 tablespoons vegetable oil

2 tablespoons whole-egg mayonnaise

2 tablespoons roasted, salted peanuts, chopped coarsely

BAO

2 cups (300g) self-raising flour

1 teaspoon baking powder

½ teaspoon caster (superfine) sugar

¼ teaspoon table salt

1 cup (250ml) light coconut milk

vegetable oil, for brushing

PINEAPPLE AND CUCUMBER SALAD

250g (8 ounces) pineapple, sliced thinly

2 lebanese cucumbers (260g), sliced thinly

1 tablespoon rice wine vinegar

1 fresh long red chilli, sliced thinly

1 clove garlic, crushed

1 cup loosely packed fresh coriander (cilantro) leaves

1 Place tofu on a small wire rack over a tray, top with a second tray (or plate); weight with cans of food. Stand 30 minutes or until tofu is a firmer texture.

2 Meanwhile, make bao, then make pineapple and cucumber salad.

3 Cut pressed tofu crossways into 8 slices. Dust with five spice and chilli; season with salt. Heat oil in a large non-stick frying pan over high heat; cook tofu, in batches, for 2 minutes each side or until golden.

4 Spread bao with mayonnaise; fill with tofu, salad and peanuts.

bao Cut eight 12cm (4¾-inch) squares from baking paper. Sift flour, baking powder, sugar and salt into a large bowl. Add coconut milk; stir with a fork until just combined. Turn dough onto a lightly floured surface; knead gently for 1 minute or until smooth. Divide dough into eight pieces; roll out each piece into a 15cm (6-inch) long oval. Brush half of each oval lightly with oil; fold in half crossways. Place each bao on a square of baking paper; cover loosely with plastic wrap. Cook bao in two batches in a large steamer over a saucepan of simmering water for 8 minutes or until cooked through.

pineapple and cucumber salad Combine ingredients in a medium bowl; season with salt.

tip Press the tofu up to a day ahead; keep covered in the fridge.

CHINESE ROAST DUCK WITH GREEN ONION PANCAKES

PREP + COOK TIME 2 HOURS 40 MINUTES (+ STANDING) **SERVES** 8

2kg (4-pound) whole duck

1.25 litres (5 cups) boiling water

4 cups (600g) plain (all-purpose) flour

2 tablespoons sesame oil

6 green onions (scallions), sliced thinly

⅓ cup (80ml) vegetable oil

2 lebanese cucumbers (260g), cut into batons

PLUM SAUCE

1 cup (300g) plum sauce

1 tablespoon caster (superfine) sugar

¼ cup (60ml) white vinegar

1 tablespoon soy sauce

4 star anise

1 cinnamon stick

1 orange (240g), rind peeled in long strips

1 cup (250ml) water

1 Preheat oven to 200°C/400°F.

2 Pierce duck skin at 5cm (2-inch) intervals with a metal skewer; place duck in a bowl. Pour 3 cups of the boiling water over duck. Drain, then pat dry with paper towel. Place duck on a wire rack over a large roasting pan lined with foil.

3 Make plum sauce.

4 Place reserved rind from plum sauce in duck cavity; secure with a skewer. Brush duck with plum sauce reserved for brushing; roast about 50 minutes, basting regularly. Cover duck loosely with foil; roast a further 30 minutes or until juices run clear when the thickest part of a thigh is pierced with a skewer. Rest duck, loosely covered with foil, 20 minutes.

5 Meanwhile, process flour. With motor operating, slowly add the remaining boiling water, processing until a dough forms. Place dough in a lightly greased bowl, cover with plastic wrap; rest 30 minutes.

6 Divide dough into 16 pieces. Roll out each piece on a lightly floured surface into an 18cm (7¼-inch) round. Brush round with a little sesame oil, season with salt; roll into a log. Coil the log, flatten and reroll into an 18cm (7¼-inch) round. Brush rounds with a little more sesame oil; top each with 1½ tablespoons of green onions. Roll up again into a log, twist into a coil, flatten and roll into a 16cm (6-inch) round.

7 Heat 1 teaspoon of the vegetable oil in a non-stick frying pan over medium heat; cook pancakes, for 2 minutes each side or until browned. Transfer to paper towel; cover to keep warm. Repeat with remaining pancakes and oil.

8 Thinly slice duck; serve with green onion pancakes, cucumber and reserved plum sauce.

plum sauce Stir ingredients in a small saucepan over low heat until sugar dissolves. Increase heat to high, bring to the boil; boil for 10 minutes or until thickened slightly. Remove rind; reserve for duck cavity. Divide mixture between two small bowls; reserve one for brushing and the other for serving.

THE GREEN ONION PANCAKE DOUGH (STEP 5) AND THE
PLUM SAUCE CAN BOTH BE MADE A DAY AHEAD;
REFRIGERATE IN SEPARATE AIRTIGHT CONTAINERS.

YOU WILL NEED SKINLESS, BONELESS, THICK FISH FILLETS SUCH AS BLUE-EYE TREVALLA OR SNAPPER. CURRY SAUCE CAN BE MADE TO THE END OF STEP 3, UP TO 2 DAYS AHEAD; REFRIGERATE, COVERED.

SRI LANKAN SEAFOOD CURRY

PREP + COOK TIME 1 HOUR 45 MINUTES **SERVES** 20

3.5kg (7 pounds) firm white fish fillets

2kg (4 pounds) uncooked large king prawns (shrimp)

6 fresh long green chillies

4 large brown onions (1.2kg), chopped coarsely

12 cloves garlic, chopped

40g (1½-ounce) piece fresh ginger, chopped coarsely

¼ cup (60ml) olive oil

2 tablespoons ground cumin

1½ tablespoons ground turmeric

⅓ cup loosely packed fresh curry leaves

1.5kg (3 pounds) ripe tomatoes, chopped

3 cups (750ml) chicken or fish stock

1 litre (4 cups) coconut cream

2 tablespoons fish sauce

3 teaspoons caster (superfine) sugar

curry leaves, extra, to serve

TOMATO SAMBAL

5 medium ripe tomatoes (750g), cut into 1cm (½-inch) pieces

1 large red onion (300g), chopped finely

2 fresh long green chillies, seeded, chopped finely

1 tablespoon tamarind puree

2 teaspoons brown sugar

⅓ cup fresh coriander (cilantro) leaves

¾ cup (45g) coconut flakes, toasted

COCONUT RICE

800ml canned coconut milk

2⅔ cups (680ml) water

4 cups (800g) basmati rice

---

1 Cut fish into 6cm (2½-inch) pieces. Shell and devein prawns, leaving tails intact. Cover seafood, separately; refrigerate until required.

2 Remove seeds from half the chillies, then coarsely chop all chillies. Process chilli with onion, garlic and ginger until finely chopped.

3 Heat oil in a very large saucepan over medium heat; cook onion mixture, stirring, for 10 minutes or until soft. Reduce heat to low, add cumin, turmeric and curry leaves; cook, stirring, about 5 minutes. Increase heat to high, add tomatoes and stock; bring to the boil. Reduce heat; simmer about 15 minutes. Add coconut cream; simmer a further 10 minutes or until vegetables are tender and flavours are developed. Add fish sauce and sugar; season to taste.

4 Meanwhile, make tomato sambal and coconut rice.

5 Add fish to curry sauce; simmer about 2 minutes. Add prawns; simmer a further 3 minutes or until prawns and fish are just cooked through.

6 Serve curry topped with extra curry leaves, and with tomato sambal and coconut rice.

tomato sambal Combine all ingredients except coconut in a medium bowl. Season. Cover; refrigerate until needed. Just before serving, stir in coconut.

coconut rice Bring coconut milk and the water to the boil in a large saucepan over medium heat. Add rice, return just to the boil, then cover with a tight-fitting lid. Reduce heat to lowest setting; cook for 16 minutes or until rice is tender and liquid absorbed. Remove from heat; stand covered, 10 minutes. Fluff rice with a fork.

MUSHROOM SLIDERS WITH HARISSA CRÈME FRAÎCHE

PREP + COOK TIME 50 MINUTES (+ STANDING) **MAKES** 8

2 tablespoons olive oil

8 x 8cm (3¼-inch) portobello mushrooms (400g)

120g (4 ounces) vintage cheddar, sliced thinly

8 small soft white bread rolls, split

40g (1½ ounces) baby rocket (arugula) leaves

½ cup loosely packed fresh flat-leaf parsley leaves

PICKLED FENNEL

1 baby fennel bulb (120g), trimmed, sliced thinly

1 clove garlic, crushed

⅓ cup (80ml) white balsamic vinegar

2 teaspoons caster (superfine) sugar

1 tablespoon fresh thyme leaves

HARISSA CRÈME FRAÎCHE

½ cup (120g) crème fraîche

2 teaspoons harissa paste

2 teaspoons lemon juice

1 Make pickled fennel.

2 Divide oil between two large non-stick frying pans, heat over medium heat. Divide mushrooms between pans; cook, covered, for 5 minutes each side or until golden and tender. For the last 2 minutes of cooking time, top mushrooms with cheddar until melted.

3 Meanwhile, make harissa crème fraîche.

4 Spread harissa crème fraîche on roll halves. Sandwich with mushrooms, pickled fennel, rocket and parsley.

pickled fennel Combine ingredients in a medium bowl; stand 30 minutes. Before serving, drain fennel mixture; discard liquid.

harissa crème fraîche Combine ingredients in a small bowl. Season to taste.

tips Try to choose mushrooms that are the same size as the rolls, otherwise you may need to double the number of mushrooms. You can reserve the fennel fronds when trimming the fennel and include in your sliders, if you like.

HARISSA CRÈME FRAÎCHE CAN BE
MADE A DAY AHEAD; REFRIGERATE
IN AN AIRTIGHT CONTAINER.

JERK FISH TACOS WITH SLAW AND AVOCADO CREAM

PREP + COOK TIME 30 MINUTES **SERVES** 16

625g (1¼ pounds) firm white fish fillets, cut diagonally into 1.5cm (¾-inch) wide, 12cm (4¾-inch) long strips

1 teaspoon ground allspice

½ teaspoon dried thyme

1½ teaspoons cayenne pepper

1 teaspoon ground cinnamon

1½ tablespoons garlic powder

¼ cup (60ml) olive oil

2 medium avocados (500g)

½ cup (120g) sour cream

2 tablespoons lime juice

350g (11 ounces) white cabbage, shredded

2 cups loosely packed fresh coriander (cilantro) leaves

1 small red onion (100g), halved, sliced thinly

1 fresh long green chilli, seeded, sliced thinly

¼ cup (60ml) freshly squeezed orange juice

1 clove garlic, crushed

16 small (14cm) flour tortillas

1 Combine fish, allspice, thyme, cayenne pepper, cinnamon, garlic powder and oil in a medium bowl. Season. Cover; refrigerate until required.

2 Blend or process avocados, sour cream and lime juice until smooth. Season to taste.

3 Combine cabbage, coriander, onion, chilli, orange juice and garlic in a large bowl. Season to taste.

4 Heat a large, non-stick frying pan over medium heat; heat tortillas, in batches, about 15 seconds each side. Wrap tortillas in foil to keep warm.

5 Increase heat to high; cook fish in same pan, in two batches, for 4 minutes or until just cooked.

6 Serve warm tortilla filled with fish and slaw, topped with avocado cream.

tips Fish can be prepared 4 hours ahead to the end of step 1. Avocado cream and coleslaw (without the orange juice) can also be prepared 4 hours ahead; add juice to coleslaw just before serving. Jerk is both the name for a Jamaican dry or wet spice seasoning, characterised by allspice and chillies, and the method of cooking over barbecue coals. Traditionally the seasoning is rubbed over chicken, pork and fish.

CHICKEN AND CAPSICUM PIES

PREP + COOK TIME 1 HOUR 50 MINUTES (+ COOLING) **SERVES** 20

4 bunches spinach (800g), washed, trimmed

½ cup (125ml) water

¼ cup (60ml) olive oil

4 large onions (800g), halved, sliced thinly

2 fennel bulbs (600g), sliced thinly, fronds reserved

6 cloves garlic, crushed

2 cups (400g) long-grain rice

3¼ cups (810ml) chicken stock

1 tablespoon finely grated lemon rind

¼ cup fresh oregano leaves, chopped

2 barbecued chickens (1.8kg), meat shredded

1 cup (250ml) pouring cream

200g (6½ ounces) greek fetta, crumbled

1 cup (150g) pitted kalamata olives, halved

150g (4½ ounces) butter, melted

30 sheets (2 packets) fillo pastry

4 large char-grilled red capsicums (bell peppers), sliced thickly

1kg (2 pounds) Greek-style yoghurt

3 cloves garlic, crushed

2 tablespoons coarsely chopped fresh dill

2 tablespoons coarsely chopped fresh flat-leaf parsley

1 Place spinach and the water in a large saucepan over medium-high heat; cook, turning spinach with tongs until starting to wilt. Cover with a lid; cook a further 2 minutes or until just wilted. Drain well. Cool slightly, then squeeze out excess liquid.

2 Heat oil in a large saucepan over medium heat; cook onion, stirring, about 5 minutes. Add fennel and garlic; cook, stirring occasionally, for 10 minutes or until vegetables are tender. Add rice, stir to coat. Add stock; bring to the boil. Cover with a tight-fitting lid, reduce to lowest heat, cook about 16 minutes until liquid is absorbed. Stand, covered, 10 minutes. Fluff mixture with a fork; transfer to a large bowl. Cool 15 minutes. Stir in rind, oregano, chopped fennel fronds, chicken, cream, fetta, olives and spinach. Season.

3 Preheat oven to 200°C/400°F. Grease two 23cm (9¼-inch) springform pans with a little melted butter.

4 Place fillo pastry sheets on a clean work surface; cover with plastic wrap, then a damp tea towel. Brush 1 fillo sheet with a little melted butter. Fold in half lengthways and place over the base of one pan allowing pastry to extend over the side. Repeat with 11 more fillo sheets, slightly overlapping, to line the base and side of the pan. Spoon a quarter of the rice mixture into the pan. Top with half the capsicum, then another quarter of rice mixture. Fold in the overhanging pastry to enclose filling.

5 Brush another fillo sheet with a little melted butter. Top with 2 more sheets, brushing each layer with a little butter. Using the pan as a guide, with a sharp knife, cut a 23cm (9¼-inch) round from pastry. Place over pie, buttered-side up. Press down to secure.

6 Repeat steps 4 and 5 with remaining fillo, butter, rice mixture and capsicum, for second pie.

7 Bake pies for 1 hour, swapping pans halfway through cooking time, or until browned and filling is hot. Stand 10 minutes before removing from pans.

8 Meanwhile, combine remaining ingredients in a medium bowl; season to taste.

9 Serve pies with herbed yoghurt.

PIES CAN BE PREPARED UP TO THE END OF STEP 6, A DAY AHEAD. REFRIGERATE, COVERED. ALLOW A LITTLE LONGER COOKING TIME SO THE HEAT HAS TIME TO REACH THE CHILLED FILLING.

THIS RECIPE CAN BE PREPARED TO THE END OF STEP 5, UP TO 2 DAYS AHEAD.

TAMARIND AND LEMON GRASS LAMB RIBS

PREP + COOK TIME 3 HOURS 40 MINUTES (+ REFRIGERATION) **SERVES 6**

½ cup (150g) firmly packed tamarind pulp

½ cup (125ml) boiling water

1 tablespoon vegetable oil

2kg (4 pounds) lamb ribs

1 litre (4 cups) chicken stock

180g (5½ ounces) dark palm sugar, grated

½ cup (125ml) soy sauce

¼ cup (60ml) fish sauce

30g (1 ounce) piece fresh ginger, sliced

6 cloves garlic, unpeeled, bruised

3 fresh stalks lemon grass, trimmed, halved

½ cup fresh vietnamese mint leaves

1 fresh long green chilli, sliced thinly

2 limes (180g), quartered

1 Place tamarind pulp and the boiling water in a bowl; soak 15 minutes. Strain mixture through a fine sieve; discard solids.

2 Preheat oven to 160°C/325°F.

3 Heat oil in a large, non-stick frying pan over medium heat; cook ribs, in two batches, 3 minutes each side or until browned. Transfer to a large deep roasting pan.

4 Add tamarind liquid, stock, sugar, sauces, ginger, garlic and lemon grass to pan, cover with foil; roast about 2 hours. Remove foil; roast a further 1 hour or until meat is very tender and sauce is reduced.

5 Transfer ribs to a large bowl and cooking liquid to a medium bowl. Cover bowls with plastic wrap; refrigerate 4 hours or until fat has solidified.

6 Scoop off solidified fat from cooking liquid; discard. Place 2 cups of the cooking liquid in a deep frying pan (discard remaining liquid) over high heat. Add ribs; cook 10 minutes, turning occasionally or until sauce boils and reduces, and ribs have warmed through. Top with mint and chilli; serve with lime.

tips If vietnamese mint is unavailable you can use spearmint leaves instead. You can serve this recipe with jasmine rice, if you like; you will need to cook 1¼ cups (250g) rice to serve six.

SLOW-ROASTED PORK BELLY WITH CRUSHED KUMARA

PREP + COOK TIME 3 HOURS 45 MINUTES (+ REFRIGERATION) SERVES 20

You will need to start this recipe the day before.

4 large brown onions (800g), unpeeled, each cut crossways into three slices

2 x 2.5kg (5-pound) pieces boneless pork belly, rind scored, patted dry

1 cup (250ml) chicken stock

1 cup (250ml) water

⅔ cup (160ml) extra virgin olive oil

1½ tablespoons sea salt

3kg (6 pounds) kumara (orange sweet potato), peeled, chopped coarsely

½ cup finely chopped fresh flat-leaf parsley

2 tablespoons finely chopped fresh chives

1 tablespoon finely chopped fresh oregano

PICKLED GRAPES

1 cup (250ml) red wine vinegar

1 cup (110g) caster (superfine) sugar

2 star anise

700g (1½ pounds) red grapes, cut into small clusters

1 small red onion (100g), halved, sliced thinly

½ cup finely chopped fresh flat-leaf parsley

1 teaspoon fennel seeds, crushed

2 tablespoons extra virgin olive oil

1 Make pickled grapes a day ahead.

2 Preheat oven to 240°C/475°F.

3 Divide onions between two large roasting pans; place pork, rind-side up, on onions. Divide stock and the water between pans, avoiding the pork. Rub 1 tablespoon of oil and half the salt onto the rind of each piece of pork.

4 Roast pork for 40 minutes or until rind starts to crackle around the edges. Reduce oven to 160°C/325°F; roast a further 2½ hours, swapping pans halfway through cooking time, or until pork is tender. (If the rind needs more crackling, increase the oven to 240°C/475°F and cook until well crackled.) Rest pork, uncovered, for 20 minutes.

5 Meanwhile, cook kumara in two large saucepans of boiling water for 20 minutes or until tender; drain well. Return all kumara to one pan with ¼ cup of the oil; season to taste. Crush roughly with a potato masher; spoon into a serving dish. Cover to keep warm.

6 Combine herbs, remaining oil and reserved grape pickling liquid in a small bowl. Season. Drizzle over crushed kumara.

7 Serve sliced pork and crackling with pan juices, crushed kumara and pickled grapes.

pickled grapes Stir vinegar, sugar and star anise in a medium saucepan over medium heat, until sugar dissolves and mixture boils. Reduce heat; simmer about 1 minute. Add grapes; simmer about 1 minute. Cool. Refrigerate, covered, overnight. Strain grapes, reserving ¼ cup pickling liquid. Combine grapes with remaining ingredients in a medium bowl. Season.

THE DAY BEFORE YOU COOK THE PORK, PAT DRY WITH PAPER TOWEL AND LEAVE UNCOVERED IN THE FRIDGE. THIS WILL DRY THE SKIN OUT A LITTLE WHICH WILL ASSIST WITH CRACKLING.

COCONUT AND PRAWN FRITTERS WITH ASIAN SALAD

PREP + COOK TIME 45 MINUTES (+ STANDING) SERVES 6

200g (6½ ounces) rice flour

1 teaspoon ground turmeric

¾ cup (180ml) coconut milk

½ cup (125ml) water

650g (1¼ pounds) uncooked medium shelled prawns (shrimp), chopped roughly

vegetable oil, for deep-frying

1 butter (boston) lettuce (120g), leaves trimmed

2 medium carrots (345g), cut into matchsticks

½ small daikon radish (200g), cut into matchsticks

1½ cups (100g) bean sprouts

1 cup firmly packed fresh coriander (cilantro) leaves

1 cup firmly packed fresh mint leaves

DIPPING SAUCE

2 tablespoons lime juice

2 tablespoons water

2 tablespoons fish sauce

1 tablespoon caster (superfine) sugar

1 fresh long red chilli, chopped finely

1 clove garlic, chopped finely

1 Place flour and turmeric in a large bowl. Whisk in coconut milk and the water to form a thick batter. Set aside 15 minutes. Stir in prawns; season with salt.

2 Meanwhile, make dipping sauce.

3 Fill a large saucepan or deep-fryer one-third full with oil; heat to 180°C/350°F (or until a cube of bread turns golden in 10 seconds). Cook ¼-cups of the fritter mixture, in batches, for 3 minutes or until crisp, golden and cooked through. Drain on paper towel.

4 Fill lettuce leaves with fritters, carrot, daikon and bean sprouts; top with herbs, roll to enclose and serve with dipping sauce.

dipping sauce Combine ingredients in a small bowl.

PEAR, SAGE AND GOAT'S CHEESE SEEDED FLATBREADS

PREP + COOK TIME 1 HOUR **SERVES** 12

2 tablespoons olive oil

3 medium firm pears (690g), halved, sliced thinly

1 large red onion (300g), sliced thinly

100g (3 ounces) mozzarella, sliced thinly

2 tablespoons pine nuts

3 teaspoons honey

2 tablespoons olive oil, extra

¼ cup loosely packed fresh sage leaves

1 clove garlic, crushed

60g (2 ounces) fresh goat's cheese, crumbled

40g (1½ ounces) baby rocket (arugula) leaves

SEEDED FLATBREADS

¾ cup (110g) spelt flour

1 teaspoon baking powder

2 tablespoons linseeds

2 tablespoons black chia seeds

½ cup (140g) Greek-style yoghurt

1   Make dough for seeded flatbreads.

2   Preheat oven to 200°C/400°F.

3   Heat oil in a large frying pan over medium heat; cook pear and onion, stirring occasionally, for 5 minutes or until pear is light golden and onion is soft. Cool.

4   Oil three large oven trays. Divide dough into three portions; roll out each portion on a lightly floured piece of baking paper into a 12cm x 42cm (4¾-inch x 16¾-inch) rectangle. Carefully lift dough on baking paper onto trays. Top with mozzarella, pear mixture and pine nuts. Season. Drizzle with honey.

5   Bake flatbreads for 15 minutes or until golden and crisp.

6   Meanwhile, heat extra oil in a small frying pan over high heat, carefully add sage leaves; cook for 30 seconds or until crisp. Remove sage with a slotted spoon; drain on paper towel. Add garlic to pan; cook, stirring, for 1 minute or until fragrant. Remove from heat; reserve for serving.

7   Serve flatbreads topped with goat's cheese, sage leaves and rocket. Drizzle with reserved garlic oil.

seeded flatbreads Sift flour and baking powder into a medium bowl; stir in seeds. Season. Add yoghurt; stir with a butter knife to combine. Knead dough in a bowl for 1 minute.

DOUGH CAN BE MADE A DAY
AHEAD. PEAR AND ONION
MIXTURE CAN BE COOKED
4 HOURS AHEAD; REFRIGERATE
IN AN AIRTIGHT CONTAINER.

BARBECUED SALMON WITH SALSA CRIOLLA

PREP + COOK TIME 40 MINUTES **SERVES** 8

2 teaspoons sea salt flakes

1 tablespoon extra virgin olive oil

2kg (4-pound) salmon fillet, skin on, pin-boned

2 tablespoons coarsely chopped fresh flat-leaf parsley

2 cloves garlic, crushed

lemon cheeks, to serve

SALSA CRIOLLA

350g (11 ounces) baby heirloom tomatoes, sliced or quartered

250g (8 ounces) cherry tomatoes, quartered

½ medium red onion (85g), chopped finely

2 tablespoons extra virgin olive oil

1 tablespoon red wine vinegar

⅓ cup loosely packed fresh coriander (cilantro) leaves

1 Make salsa criolla.

2 Preheat a covered barbecue with all burners on low and hood closed until temperature reaches 200°C/400°F, or follow manufacturer's instructions.

3 Combine salt and half the oil in a small bowl; rub mixture on skin side of salmon. Combine parsley, garlic and remaining oil in a small bowl; rub mixture on flesh side of salmon. Season.

4 Barbecue salmon on grills, skin-side down, in covered barbecue. Turn burners off underneath salmon and turn other burners to high. Cook on covered barbecue for 20 minutes or until cooked as desired (salmon is best served medium-rare in the thickest part).

5 Serve salmon with salsa criolla and lemon cheeks.

salsa criolla Combine all ingredients, except coriander, in a medium bowl. Season to taste. Just before serving, add coriander; toss to combine.

tips Whole white fish could be used instead of the salmon, if you like. Cut slits into the thickest part of the fish and rub the oil mixture into the cuts.

PAPRIKA CHICKEN WITH CHILLI SAUCE

PREP + COOK TIME 1 HOUR 20 MINUTES SERVES 6

2 x 1kg (2-pound) chickens

1 punnet micro coriander (cilantro)

CHILLI SAUCE

250g (8 ounces) fresh long red chillies, seeded, chopped

1 tablespoon caster (superfine) sugar

2 teaspoons sea salt flakes

½ cup (125ml) white vinegar

¼ cup (60ml) water

OREGANO AND SMOKED PAPRIKA RUB

1 tablespoon smoked paprika

4 cloves garlic, crushed

2 tablespoons chopped fresh oregano leaves

2 tablespoons extra virgin olive oil

3 teaspoons sea salt flakes

1 Make chilli sauce.

2 Preheat a covered barbecue with all burners on low and hood closed until temperature reaches 240°C/475°F, or follow manufacturer's instructions.

3 Make oregano and smoked paprika rub.

4 Cut chickens along both sides of backbone with kitchen scissors; remove and discard backbones. Turn chickens over; press down on breastbone to flatten slightly. Place chickens, skin-side up in one large ovenproof dish or two small ones; rub all over with oregano and smoked paprika rub.

5 Place dish in centre of barbecue; turn burners off underneath dish, leaving other burners on low. Cook in covered barbecue for 40 minutes or until browned and cooked through.

6 Serve chickens cut into portions, topped with chilli sauce and micro coriander.

chilli sauce Stir ingredients in a small saucepan over high heat; bring to the boil. Reduce heat; simmer, covered, for 8 minutes or until chilli is tender. Cool 5 minutes. Blend sauce until smooth; season to taste. Strain sauce into a jar. (Makes 1¼ cups.)

oregano and smoked paprika rub Combine ingredients in a small bowl.

tips Chilli sauce can be made a day ahead; refrigerate in an airtight container. To make the chicken easier and faster to barbecue it is first flattened by removing the backbone, a cooking technique known as spatchcocking or butterflying.

SMALL DISPOSABLE ALUMINIUM BAKING DISHES WORK WELL FOR THIS RECIPE. CHICKENS CAN ALSO BE ROASTED IN THE OVEN ON SHALLOW OVEN TRAYS AT 220° C / 425° F FOR 40 MINUTES.

NEW-YORK CUT STEAK (BONELESS SIRLOIN), EYE FILLET, RIB-EYE AND RUMP STEAKS ARE ALL SUITABLE FOR THIS RECIPE.

BARBECUED STEAKS WITH CORN SALAD

PREP + COOK TIME 1 HOUR SERVES 8

4 corn cobs (1.6kg), trimmed

⅓ cup (80ml) olive oil

8 x 250g (8-ounce) scotch fillet steaks

1 medium red onion (170g), chopped finely

250g (8 ounces) grape tomatoes, halved

⅓ cup (80ml) lime juice

⅔ cup fresh coriander (cilantro) sprigs

ANCHOVY BUTTER

160g (5 ounces) butter, softened

8 drained anchovy fillets, chopped finely

2 cloves garlic, crushed

¼ cup finely chopped fresh coriander (cilantro)

1 Make anchovy butter.

2 Meanwhile, brush corn with 2 teaspoons of the oil; cook on a heated barbecue grill plate (or chargrill pan or grill), turning, for 15 minutes or until lightly charred and tender. Cool 5 minutes.

3 Brush steaks all over with 1½ tablespoons of the oil; cook on barbecue for 2 minutes each side for medium rare or until cooked as desired. Cover steaks; rest 5 minutes.

4 Combine onion, tomato, juice and remaining oil in a large bowl; season. Cut kernels from corn, keeping kernels together in large pieces. Add to bowl with coriander; toss gently to combine.

5 Serve steaks topped with sliced anchovy butter and corn salad.

anchovy butter Mash ingredients in a small bowl with a fork until well combined. Roll mixture tightly in plastic wrap to make a log; refrigerate until firm.

tips Make the anchovy butter a day ahead and refrigerate, or even a month ahead and freeze it.

RIGATONI WITH OVEN-ROASTED VEGETABLES

PREP + COOK TIME 1 HOUR SERVES 8

2 medium red onions (340g), cut into wedges

500g (1 pound) yellow patty-pan squash, halved

24 baby zucchini (240g), halved lengthways

⅓ cup (80ml) extra virgin olive oil

550g (1 pound) baby truss roma (egg) tomatoes

⅔ cup (160ml) red wine

1.4kg (2¾ pounds) bottled tomato pasta sauce

1kg (2 pounds) rigatoni pasta

⅔ cup loosely packed fresh baby basil leaves

1 Preheat oven to 220°C/425°F.

2 Place onion, squash and zucchini on a large oven tray; drizzle with ¼ cup (60ml) of the oil. Roast about 20 minutes. Add tomatoes to tray, roast a further 10 minutes or until onion is golden and softened and tomatoes begin to split. Remove tomatoes from tray; cover to keep warm.

3 Heat remaining oil in a large frying pan over medium-high heat; add roasted vegetables, cook, stirring, about 1 minute. Add wine; cook until reduced by half. Add sauce; bring to the boil. Reduce heat to low; cook for 20 minutes or until sauce is reduced slightly. Season to taste.

4 Meanwhile, cook pasta in a large saucepan of boiling salted water for 8 minutes or until just tender; drain.

5 Serve pasta topped with sauce, roasted tomatoes and basil.

CHORIZO, CHICKPEA AND PUMPKIN SALAD

PREP + COOK TIME 1 HOUR 20 MINUTES **SERVES** 8

1kg (2 pounds) butternut pumpkin halves

1 teaspoon ground cumin

1 teaspoon smoked paprika

2 tablespoons extra virgin olive oil

1 large red onion (300g), cut into wedges

2 x 125g (4-ounce) cured chorizo sausages, sliced thickly

400g (12½ ounces) canned chickpeas (garbanzo beans), rinsed, drained

1 fresh long red chilli, sliced thickly

½ cup loosely packed fresh flat-leaf parsley leaves

½ cup loosely packed fresh coriander (cilantro) sprigs

SHERRY VINEGAR DRESSING

2 tablespoons extra virgin olive oil

1 tablespoon light olive or vegetable oil

1 tablespoon sherry vinegar

1 clove garlic, crushed

1 Preheat a covered barbecue with all burners on low and hood closed until temperature reaches 220°C/425°F, or follow manufacturer's instructions.

2 Peel pumpkin; cut pumpkin crossways into 2cm (¾-inch) slices, then cut each slice into four pieces.

3 Combine cumin, paprika and oil in a small bowl. Toss pumpkin with half the spice mixture in a medium ovenproof dish; season. Add onion to dish. Place dish on barbecue; turn burners off underneath dish, leaving the other burners on low. Cook pumpkin and onion in covered barbecue for 40 minutes or until almost tender.

4 Combine chorizo, chickpeas and chilli in a large bowl with remaining spice mixture. Add to baking dish with pumpkin; cook in covered barbecue for 20 minutes or until chorizo and pumpkin are browned and tender.

5 Meanwhile, make sherry vinegar dressing.

6 Drizzle dressing over salad, then add herbs; toss gently to combine.

sherry vinegar dressing Place ingredients in a screw-top jar; shake well. Season to taste.

tips Disposable aluminium baking dishes available from supermarkets are great to use for cooking on the barbecue. This recipe can also be roasted in a 200°C/400°F oven for the same cooking time.

SUMAC CHILLI LAMB

PREP + COOK TIME 45 MINUTES SERVES 8

2 large red onions (600g), cut into wedges

2 large red capsicums (bell peppers) (700g), cut into strips

800g (1½ pounds) dutch (baby) carrots, trimmed, unpeeled

6 finger eggplants (960g), sliced lengthways

¼ cup (60ml) olive oil

1.6kg (3¼ pounds) lamb backstraps, trimmed

2 tablespoons olive oil, extra

¼ cup (25g) sumac

2 teaspoons dried chilli flakes

200g (6½ ounces) baby rocket (arugula)

½ cup (125ml) lemon juice

⅓ cup (80ml) extra virgin olive oil

WHITE BEAN PUREE

1.6kg (3¼ pounds) canned cannellini beans, rinsed, drained

2 cloves garlic, crushed

½ cup (125ml) lemon juice

⅔ cup (160ml) olive oil

1 Preheat oven to 180°C/350°F. Line a large roasting tray with baking paper.

2 Place vegetables on tray, drizzle with olive oil and season; toss to combine. Roast for 30 minutes or until tender.

3 Meanwhile, rub lamb with extra olive oil then roll in sumac and chilli. Cook lamb on heated grill plate (or grill or barbecue) over medium-high heat, turning occasionally, for 4 minutes for medium rare or until cooked to your liking. Cover with foil; rest for 5 minutes.

4 Meanwhile, make white bean puree.

5 Add rocket to vegetables, drizzle with juice and extra virgin olive oil; toss to combine. Spoon half the bean puree among plates, top with vegetable mixture. Cut lamb into thin slices; place on salad, drizzle with remaining bean puree.

white bean puree Process ingredients until smooth, adding a little water if necessary, until mixture reaches a dipping consistency. Season to taste.

WE USED FLATHEAD FOR THE FIRM WHITE FISH FILLETS. PIE CAN BE MADE TO THE END OF STEP 4 UP TO 6 HOURS AHEAD.

CREAMY PRAWN AND FISH PIE

PREP + COOK TIME 1 HOUR 30 MINUTES SERVES 8

1 litre (4 cups) milk

1 medium leek (350g), sliced thinly

1 trimmed celery stick (100g), sliced thinly

400g (12½ ounces) firm white fish fillets, skin removed, cut into 3cm (1¼-inch) pieces

400g (12½ ounces) salmon fillets, skin removed, cut into 3cm (1¼-inch) pieces

80g (2½ ounces) butter

½ cup (75g) plain (all-purpose) flour

1 cup (120g) grated cheddar

400g (12½ ounces) uncooked peeled medium king prawns (shrimp)

400g (12½ ounces) smoked fish (such as trout, haddock or cod), skin removed, flaked

2 tablespoons finely chopped fresh dill

2 teaspoons finely grated lemon rind

1 tablespoon lemon juice

30g (1 ounce) butter, chopped finely, extra

2 sprigs fresh dill, extra

MASH

1.2kg (2½ pounds) desiree potatoes

⅓ cup (80ml) milk, warmed

90g (3 ounces) butter, chopped

1 Place milk, leek and celery in a large saucepan over medium heat; bring to a simmer. Add fish; simmer, uncovered, over low heat, for 10 minutes or until fish is cooked through. Strain milk mixture over a large bowl, reserve. Transfer fish and vegetables to a medium bowl.

2 Meanwhile, make mash.

3 Preheat oven to 180°C/350°F.

4 Heat butter in a saucepan over medium-high heat, add flour; cook, stirring, until mixture thickens and bubbles. Gradually add reserved milk; whisk until mixture boils and thickens. Add cheddar; stir until smooth. Add cooked fish, prawns, smoked fish, dill, rind and juice; stir to combine. Season. Remove from heat.

5 Transfer fish mixture to a 3-litre (12-cup) ovenproof dish; top evenly with mash. Using a fork, swirl mash in a decorative pattern; dot with extra butter.

6 Bake pie for 45 minutes or until heated through and mash is golden. Serve topped with extra dill.

mash Boil, steam or microwave potatoes until tender; drain. Mash potato with warmed milk and butter in a large bowl until smooth; season to taste.

PROSCIUTTO AND PEA TART

PREP + COOK TIME 1 HOUR 30 MINUTES (+ COOLING) **SERVES** 8

500g (1 pound) packaged ready-steamed brown basmati rice

⅓ cup (50g) pepitas (pumpkin seed kernels)

1½ cups (120g) finely grated pecorino cheese

3 eggs

1 teaspoon sea salt flakes

500g (1 pound) fresh ricotta

150g (4½ ounces) soft goat's cheese

¼ cup (60ml) milk

1 tablespoon dijon mustard

1 clove garlic, crushed

50g (1½ ounces) sugar snap peas, trimmed

80g (2½ ounces) frozen broad (fava) beans, peeled

50g (1½ ounces) snow peas, trimmed

40g (1½ ounces) frozen peas

1 teaspoon olive oil

4 slices prosciutto (60g)

100g (3 ounces) goat's cheese, extra

½ cup lightly packed snowpea tendrils (optional)

DRESSING

1 tablespoon extra virgin olive oil

3 teaspoons white wine vinegar

1 Preheat oven to 200°C/400°F. Grease a 23cm (9-inch) round springform pan.

2 Process rice, pepitas and half the pecorino until rice is finely chopped. Add 1 egg and half the salt; process until mixture forms a coarse dough.

3 Using damp hands, press rice dough over base and side of the pan, stopping 5mm (¼ inch) from the top. Bake for 30 minutes or until golden and dry to the touch.

4 Meanwhile, process ricotta, goat's cheese, milk, mustard and garlic with remaining pecorino, eggs and salt until smooth.

5 Pour cheese mixture into warm rice crust. Reduce oven to 180°C/350°F; bake for 30 minutes or until a skewer inserted into the centre comes out clean. Cool 1 hour.

6 Meanwhile, cook sugar snap peas in a large saucepan of boiling water for 1 minute. Add broad beans, snow peas and frozen peas; cook a further minute or until tender. Drain, then refresh in ice-cold water.

7 Heat oil in a large non-stick frying pan over medium heat; cook prosciutto for 3 minutes or until golden. Drain on paper towel. Break into smaller pieces.

8 Make dressing. Place peas and beans in a small bowl with three-quarters of the dressing; toss gently to combine.

9 Just before serving, arrange pea salad, extra goat's cheese, prosciutto and snowpea tendrils on tart; drizzle with remaining dressing. Season with freshly ground black pepper.

dressing Place ingredients in a screw-top jar; shake well. Season to taste.

tip Don't be concerned if the cooked tart has small cracks in the top; these will be covered by the salad.

THE TART AND DRESSING CAN BE MADE A DAY
AHEAD. REFRIGERATE IN SEPARATE AIRTIGHT CONTAINERS.

SIDE *Plates*

LETTUCE WEDGES WITH CREAMY LEMON DRESSING

PREP TIME 20 MINUTES **SERVES** 8

300g (9½ ounces) sour cream

1 cup (300g) whole-egg mayonnaise

1 teaspoon finely grated lemon rind

1½ tablespoons lemon juice

½ medium brown onion (80g)

4 baby cos (romaine) lettuce (720g)

¼ cup (20g) fried asian shallots

¼ cup loosely packed fresh flat-leaf parsley leaves

1 Place sour cream, mayonnaise, rind and juice in a medium bowl. Coarsely grate onion into a small bowl. Press down on onion to extract as much juice as possible; discard onion, reserve onion juice. Add onion juice to sour cream mixture, stir to combine; season.

2 Remove outer leaves from lettuce; discard root end. Cut each lettuce into quarters lengthways (if necessary, push a 20cm (8-inch) bamboo skewer through the leaves to hold them together).

3 Arrange lettuce wedges on a large platter. Drizzle with dressing; scatter with shallots and parsley.

MEXICAN-STYLE BARBECUED CORN

PREP + COOK TIME 35 MINUTES SERVES 8

1 tablespoon chipotle chillies in adobo sauce

2 teaspoons lime juice

1½ cups (450g) whole-egg mayonnaise

2 tablespoons pepitas (pumpkin seed kernels)

½ teaspoon smoked spanish paprika

½ teaspoon ground cumin

8 cobs corn (2kg), in husks

⅔ cup (50g) finely grated parmesan

4 limes (360g), cut into cheeks

1 Process chillies in adobo sauce with juice and mayonnaise until smooth.

2 Stir pepitas in a dry frying pan over medium-low heat for 3 minutes or until browned lightly. Add paprika and cumin, stir a further 15 seconds. Transfer to a small bowl.

3 Cook corn in husks in a large saucepan of boiling salted water for 6 minutes or until almost tender. Drain; cool in husks. Peel back the corn husks; remove and discard the silks. Tie the husks back with kitchen string.

4 Heat a barbecue or chargrill pan over medium heat; cook corn, turning, for 5 minutes or until lightly charred.

5 Place corn on a platter, spoon a little chipotle mayonnaise on cobs; sprinkle with parmesan, then pepita mixture. Serve with lime cheeks and remaining chipotle mayonnaise.

LABNE CAN BE MADE 5 DAYS AHEAD. REFRIGERATE, COVERED WITH OLIVE OIL, IN A SMALL SHALLOW CONTAINER. DRAIN BEFORE USING. YOU CAN USE 150G (4½ OUNCES) CRUMBLED FETTA OR SOFT GOAT'S CHEESE INSTEAD OF LABNE.

TOMATO SALAD WITH LABNE AND SEEDS

PREP + COOK TIME 35 MINUTES (+ REFRIGERATION)   SERVES 8

You will need to start this recipe the day before.

2 teaspoons sesame seeds

2 teaspoons sunflower seeds

2 tablespoons coarsely chopped pistachios

2 teaspoons ground cumin

1 teaspoon sea salt flakes

1kg (2 pounds) large and small heirloom tomatoes

½ cup (60g) sicilian green olives

½ small red onion (50g), sliced thinly

3 cups (350g) firmly packed watercress sprigs

¼ cup loosely packed fresh coriander (cilantro) sprigs

LABNE

1 teaspoon sea salt flakes

500g (1 pound) Greek-style yoghurt

DRESSING

¼ cup (60ml) extra virgin olive oil

1½ tablespoons lemon juice

1 clove garlic, quartered

1 Make labne, then dressing.

2 Stir seeds, nuts, cumin and salt in a dry medium frying pan over low heat for 5 minutes or until fragrant. Remove from pan; cool.

3 Halve or thickly slice some of the larger tomatoes; place all tomatoes in a large bowl. Slice cheeks from olives close to the pits; discard pits. Add olives to bowl with onion, watercress, coriander and half the dressing; toss gently to combine. Season to taste.

4 Serve tomato salad topped with labne and seed mixture; drizzle with remaining dressing.

labne Stir salt into yoghurt in a small bowl. Line a sieve with two layers of muslin (or a clean, unused open weave cloth); place sieve over a deep bowl or jug. Spoon yoghurt mixture into sieve, gather cloth and tie into a ball with kitchen string. Refrigerate for 24 hours or until thick, gently squeezing occasionally to encourage the liquid to drain. Discard liquid. Roll or shape tablespoons of labne into balls.

dressing Place ingredients in a screw-top jar, season to taste; shake well. Stand at least 20 minutes or refrigerate overnight. Discard garlic before using.

serving suggestion Serve with wholemeal turkish or afghan bread.

CRUNCHY MUNG BEAN AND CORIANDER SALAD

PREP + COOK TIME 10 MINUTES **SERVES** 8

2 tablespoons sunflower seeds

2 tablespoons pepitas (pumpkin seed kernels)

85g (3 ounces) fresh coriander (cilantro), roots and stems attached

3 green onions (scallions), sliced thinly

¼ teaspoon ground coriander

¼ teaspoon ground cumin

¼ cup (60ml) extra virgin olive oil

¼ cup (60ml) lime juice

2 lebanese cucumbers (260g)

2 medium egg (plum) tomatoes (150g)

400g (12½ ounces) crunchy combo sprouted legumes

1 Stir seeds in a small frying pan, over medium heat, until toasted lightly. Cool.

2 Wash fresh coriander well; drain and pat dry. Reserve 1 cup loosely packed coriander leaves. Scrape and clean coriander roots. Blend or process coriander roots, stems and remaining coriander leaves with one-third each of the onion, spices, oil and juice; process until finely chopped. Season to taste.

3 Halve cucumbers and tomatoes; remove seeds, then cut into 1cm (½-inch) pieces.

4 Place seeds, coriander dressing, cucumber and tomato in a large bowl with sprouts and remaining onion, spices, oil and juice; toss gently to combine. Season to taste. Serve immediately.

serving suggestion Crusty bread.

THE DRESSING DISCOLOURS QUICKLY,
SO MAKE IT CLOSE TO SERVING.

WARM BEETROOT AND HEIRLOOM CARROT SALAD

PREP + COOK TIME 1 HOUR **SERVES** 8

1kg (2 pounds) golden baby beetroot (beets), trimmed

1kg (2 pounds) red baby beetroot (beets), trimmed

1.6kg (3¼ pounds) baby carrots, trimmed

1.6kg (3¼ pounds) baby purple carrots, trimmed

2 large red onions (600g), cut into thick wedges

1 tablespoon dijon mustard

1 cup loosely packed fresh mint leaves

2 x 180g (5½-ounce) tubs persian fetta, drained, crumbled

DRESSING

1 cup (250ml) olive oil

½ cup (125ml) red wine vinegar

2 tablespoons honey

1 Make dressing.

2 Preheat oven to 200°C/400°F. Line two large oven trays with baking paper.

3 Scrub beetroot and carrots. Divide beetroot, carrot and onion between trays. Spoon half the dressing over vegetables; toss to coat. Season. Roast for 45 minutes or until vegetables are tender; cool slightly. Peel beetroot; cut in half (or quarters if large). Cut carrots in half lengthways.

4 Stir mustard into remaining dressing.

5 Arrange vegetables on a platter; top with mint and remaining dressing. Serve warm topped wtih fetta.

dressing Whisk ingredients together in a small bowl; season to taste.

tip If you don't have oven trays large enough to roast all the vegetables at once, cook them in batches; cover roasted vegetables to keep warm.

SAGE AND OLIVE SAUTEED POTATOES

PREP + COOK TIME 1 HOUR **SERVES** 8

500g (1 pound) baby new potatoes, halved

1kg (2 pounds) kipfler (fingerling) potatoes, scrubbed, halved lengthways

⅔ cup (160ml) extra virgin olive oil

1 bulb garlic, halved crossways

½ cup loosely packed fresh sage leaves

½ cup (80g) kalamata olives, halved, pitted

2 medium lemons (280g), rind peeled in wide strips

1 Preheat oven to 160°C/325°F.

2 Place baby potatoes in a large saucepan with enough water to cover. Bring to the boil; boil about 5 minutes. Remove potatoes with a slotted spoon; drain. Place potatoes, cut-side up, on a clean tea towel to dry.

3 Cook kipfler potatoes in same water, return water to the boil; boil about 5 minutes. Drain. Place potatoes, cut-side up, on the tea towel to dry.

4 Meanwhile, heat oil with garlic in a small saucepan over the lowest heat about 20 minutes. Increase heat to medium. Add sage, in two batches, for 30 seconds or until crisp. Remove with a slotted spoon; drain on paper towel. Remove garlic from oil; reserve. Turn off the heat under oil.

5 Heat 2 tablespoons of garlic-sage oil in a large frying pan; cook one-third of the potatoes, cut-side down first, for 2 minutes, turn and cook a further minute or until deep golden. Transfer to a roasting pan; keep warm in the oven. Repeat cooking with another 2 tablespoons of oil and a third of potatoes; add to the roasting pan. Repeat cooking with 1 tablespoon of oil, remaining potatoes, olives and rind.

6 Add potatoes, olives, rind and reserved garlic to the roasting pan, season to taste; toss to combine. Serve topped with sage.

tips Potatoes should be slightly undercooked after boiling. Remaining garlic-infused oil can be used in salad dressings.

LEFT OVER GARLIC FRYING OIL CAN BE USED IN STIR-FRIES OR FOR ROASTING VEGETABLES.

GAI LAN WITH OYSTER SAUCE

PREP + COOK TIME 10 MINUTES **SERVES** 8

½ cup (125ml) peanut oil

8 cloves garlic, sliced thinly

1.25kg (2½ pounds) gai lan, trimmed, halved

⅓ cup (80ml) oyster sauce

¼ cup (60ml) light soy sauce

1 fresh long red chilli, sliced thinly

1 Place oil and garlic in a wok over medium heat. Once oil starts to sizzle, stir garlic continuously for 2 minutes or until golden. Remove garlic immediately with a slotted spoon; drain on paper towel. Remove wok from heat; reserve 2 tablespoons oil from the wok, discard remaining.

2 Cook gai lan stems in a large saucepan of boiling water about 1 minute. Add gai lan leaves; cook a further 30 seconds or until leaves and stems are almost tender. Drain well.

3 Heat reserved oil in wok over high heat, add gai lan and sauces; stir-fry for 2 minutes or until mixture is heated through. Serve topped with fried garlic and chilli.

ROAST PUMPKIN AND PARSNIP WITH HUMMUS DRESSING

PREP + COOK TIME 55 MINUTES SERVES 10

500g (1 pound) jap pumpkin, cut into wedges

4 small parsnips (320g), halved lengthways

¼ cup (60ml) olive oil

1 tablespoon cumin seeds

2 teaspoons ground coriander

800g (1½ pounds) canned chickpeas (garbanzo beans), rinsed, drained

200g (6½ ounces) sourdough bread, torn into small chunks

¼ cup (60ml) olive oil, extra

½ cup loosely packed fresh flat-leaf parsley leaves, torn

½ cup loosely packed fresh mint leaves, torn

HUMMUS DRESSING

1 tablespoon tahini

½ cup (120g) sour cream

2 tablespoons lemon juice

¼ teaspoon paprika

pinch cayenne pepper

¼ cup (60ml) cold water

1 Preheat oven to 220°C/425°F.

2 Place pumpkin and parsnip in a large bowl with oil, seeds and ground coriander; season. Toss to combine. Place vegetables, in a single layer, on two baking-paper-lined oven trays; reserve spiced oil in the bowl. Roast vegetables about 30 minutes, turning once during cooking.

3 Meanwhile, stir ¾ cup of chickpeas into reserved spiced oil until coated; reserve.

4 Make hummus dressing.

5 Toss bread on an oven tray with extra oil until evenly coated; season. Cook bread on separate shelf in oven for 8 minutes, stirring occasionally, or until bread is browned and crisp.

6 Add reserved chickpea mixture to vegetables; roast a further 10 minutes or until vegetables are tender. Place vegetables and chickpeas on a serving platter with bread; drizzle with dressing and scatter with herbs.

hummus dressing Blend dressing ingredients with remaining chickpeas until smooth. Season to taste.

GREEN BARLEY SALAD

PREP + COOK TIME 30 MINUTES SERVES 8

1½ cups (300g) pearl barley

1½ cups (180g) frozen peas

1½ cups (225g) shelled edamame

200g (6½ ounces) snow peas, sliced thinly

3 green onions (scallions), sliced thinly

⅔ cup loosely packed fresh mint leaves

¼ cup (60ml) extra virgin olive oil

2 tablespoons lemon juice

335g (10½ ounces) labne in olive oil, drained

1 Cook barley in a medium saucepan of salted water over medium heat for 25 minutes or until tender. Drain; rinse under cold water until cold. Drain well.
2 Meanwhile, bring a medium saucepan of salted water to the boil. Add frozen peas, edamame and snow peas; boil about 1 minute. Drain; place in a bowl of iced water until cold. Drain well.
3 Place barley and pea mixture in a shallow serving dish with onion and mint; drizzle with combined oil and juice. Toss gently to combine. Season to taste.
4 Serve salad topped with labne.

BABY BEETROOT, LENTIL AND WATERCRESS SALAD

PREP + COOK TIME 40 MINUTES **SERVES** 8

2kg (4 pounds) baby beetroot (beets)

4 cloves garlic, sliced

½ cup fresh rosemary leaves

⅓ cup (80ml) extra virgin olive oil

½ cup (125ml) balsamic vinegar

1 cup (200g) French-style green lentils

2 large pomegranates (900g)

6 cups (180g) trimmed watercress

⅔ cup (90g) roasted hazelnuts, halved

1 Preheat oven to 200°C/400°F.

2 Trim beetroot tops to 4cm (1½ inches); halve beetroot, or quarter if large. Place beetroot, garlic and rosemary in two large ovenproof dishes; drizzle with oil and vinegar. Roast, uncovered, for 30 minutes or until tender.

3 Meanwhile, cook lentils in a medium saucepan of boiling water for 25 minutes or until tender. Drain; rinse under cold water. Drain well.

4 Cut pomegranates in half crossways; hold a half, cut-side down, in the palm of your hand over a small bowl, then hit the outside firmly with a wooden spoon. The seeds should fall out easily; discard any white pith that falls out with them. Repeat with the remaining halves.

5 Place lentils, beetroot and cooking juices, watercress, half the pomegranate seeds and half the nuts in a large bowl; toss gently to combine. Season to taste. Transfer to a serving bowl; top with remaining pomegranate seeds and nuts.

tips If the beetroot leaves are fresh, you can trim, wash and reserve the smallest ones, then add to the salad with the watercress. If roasted hazelnuts are unavailable, you can roast your own. Place nuts on an oven tray; roast at 200°C/400°F for 5 minutes or until the skins begin to split. Place nuts in a clean tea towel and rub them together to remove the skin. Leave to cool.

POLENTA AND DRESSING CAN BE MADE A DAY AHEAD; REFRIGERATE, COVERED. VEGETABLES CAN BE COOKED A FEW HOURS AHEAD; KEEP WRAPPED IN A DAMP CLOTH IN THE FRIDGE.

SUPERGREENS SALAD WITH POLENTA CROÛTONS

PREP + COOK TIME 20 MINUTES (+ REFRIGERATION) SERVES 8

1 litre (4 cups) vegetable stock

1½ tablespoons finely chopped fresh rosemary leaves

2 cups (340g) instant polenta

400g (12½ ounces) broccollini, trimmed, halved

400g (12½ ounces) green beans, trimmed

340g (11 ounces) asparagus, trimmed

2 cups (240g) frozen peas

100g (3 ounces) baby spinach leaves

cooking-oil spray

200g (6½ ounces) soft blue cheese, crumbled

PICKLED SULTANA DRESSING

½ cup (80g) sultanas

⅓ cup (80ml) white wine vinegar

1 clove garlic, crushed

2 tablespoons maple syrup

2 tablespoons olive oil

1 Grease a 20cm x 30cm (8-inch x 12-inch) slice pan; line base and long sides with baking paper, extending the paper 5cm (2 inches) over sides.

2 Bring stock and rosemary to the boil in a medium saucepan. Whisking continuously, gradually add polenta; whisk for 1 minute or until thick. Pour into pan; spread evenly. Refrigerate 1 hour or until set.

3 Meanwhile, make pickled sultana dressing.

4 Cook broccollini, beans, asparagus and peas in a large saucepan of boiling salted water for 2 minutes or until just tender. Drain; refresh under cold water. Place in a large bowl with spinach.

5 Preheat grill (broiler). Lightly spray an oven tray with cooking oil.

6 Cut polenta into 48 squares; place on tray, then spray with cooking oil. Place polenta under heated grill for 3 minutes each side or until golden and crisp.

7 Add dressing to salad; toss gently to combine. Just before serving, top salad with cheese and polenta croûtons.

pickled sultana dressing Combine sultanas, vinegar, garlic and maple syrup in a small bowl. Season to taste. Stand 10 minutes. Stir in oil.

WITLOF, FENNEL AND ZUCCHINI SALAD WITH ORANGE DRESSING

PREP + COOK TIME 35 MINUTES **SERVES** 8

2 small green zucchini (180g), sliced thinly lengthways

1 tablespoon extra virgin olive oil

2 teaspoons chopped fresh oregano leaves

2 medium witlof (belgian endive) (300g), trimmed, leaves separated

1 medium fennel bulb (300g), fronds reserved, sliced thinly

2 medium oranges (480g), peeled, sliced crossways

1 medium beetroot (200g), peeled, cut into matchsticks

180g (5½-ounce) tub persian fetta, drained

ORANGE DRESSING

1 cup (250ml) freshly squeezed orange juice

1 small clove garlic, crushed

1½ tablespoons sherry vinegar

1 tablespoon olive oil

1 Make orange dressing.

2 Place zucchini, oil and oregano in a medium bowl; season, toss gently to combine.

3 Heat a barbecue (or chargrill pan or grill) to high. Barbecue zucchini for 2 minutes each side or until browned and almost tender.

4 Layer witlof, fennel, zucchini, orange and beetroot on a platter or shallow serving bowl. Season to taste. Sprinkle with fetta and drizzle with orange dressing. Top with reserved fennel fronds.

orange dressing Simmer juice in a small saucepan, uncovered, for 8 minutes or until reduced to ¼ cup. Transfer to a small bowl; whisk in garlic, vinegar and oil until combined. Season to taste.

tips As you slice or shave the fennel, drop it into a bowl of iced water to make it crisp. You will need about 6 oranges for this recipe. The dressing can be made several hours ahead; keep refrigerated. Stand at room temperature for 30 minutes and shake well before using.

ROASTED ASPARAGUS AND SMASHED POTATOES

PREP + COOK TIME 45 MINUTES **SERVES** 8

700g (1½ pounds) baby new potatoes

¼ cup (60ml) macadamia oil

340g (11 ounces) green asparagus, trimmed

340g (11 ounces) white asparagus, trimmed

¾ cup (100g) macadamias, chopped coarsely

100g (3 ounces) shaved parmesan

1 Preheat oven to 220°C/425°F.

2 Boil, steam or microwave potatoes until just tender; drain. Press warm potatoes lightly inside a clean tea towel with the palm of your hand. Place potatoes in a large shallow baking-paper-lined baking dish; season. Drizzle half the oil over potatoes.

3 Roast potatoes about 20 minutes.

4 Place asparagus on potatoes; drizzle with remaining oil, sprinkle with nuts. Roast in oven a further 5 minutes or until the edges of the potatoes are crisp and golden and asparagus is tender.

5 Serve asparagus and potatoes sprinkled with parmesan.

tip If white asparagus is unavailable, use extra green asparagus or baby carrots instead.

FATTOUSH

PREP TIME 20 MINUTES SERVES 8

360g (11½ ounces) persian fetta in oil

⅓ cup (80ml) pomegranate molasses

⅓ cup (80ml) lemon juice

2 baby cos (romaine) lettuce (360g), leaves separated, torn

2 lebanese cucumbers (260g), sliced thinly

12 red radishes (600g), sliced thinly

6 green onions (scallions), sliced thinly lengthways

2 medium green capsicums (bell peppers) (400g), cut into 2cm (¾-inch) pieces

500g (1 pound) cherry tomatoes, halved

1 cup loosely packed fresh mint leaves

100g (3 ounces) pitta crisps

1 teaspoon sumac

1 Drain oil from fetta into a jug or small bowl; reserve ½ cup.

2 Whisk pomegranate molasses, reserved fetta oil and juice in a large bowl. Season to taste. Add lettuce, cucumber, radish, onion, capsicum, tomato and mint; toss gently to combine.

3 Serve salad topped with crumbled fetta and pitta crisps; sprinkle with sumac.

tip Pitta crisps are available from some delicatessens, greengrocers and specialist food stores.

serving suggestion Serve with prawns or sliced barbecued lamb backstraps.

THE DRESSING CAN BE MADE A DAY AHEAD;
REFRIGERATE IN A SCREW-TOP JAR. ASSEMBLE
THE SALAD JUST BEFORE SERVING.

RED SALAD

PREP + COOK TIME 30 MINUTES (+ STANDING) SERVES 8

⅔ cup (160ml) tarragon vinegar

¼ cup (55g) caster (superfine) sugar

1 medium red onion (170g), halved, sliced thinly

½ medium red cabbage (750g), shredded finely

¼ cup (20g) flaked almonds

450g (14½ ounces) canned baby beetroot (beets)

¼ cup fresh chives, cut into lengths

2 small radicchios (300g), cut into thin wedges

150g (4½ ounces) goat's cheese

1 tablespoon extra virgin olive oil

1 Whisk vinegar and sugar in a large bowl until sugar is dissolved. Add onion and cabbage; toss gently to coat. Stand 30 minutes to pickle slightly. Drain in a colander; discard excess dressing. Season to taste.

2 Meanwhile, stir nuts in a small frying pan over medium heat until toasted lightly. Cool.

3 Drain beetroot; cut any larger pieces into irregular shapes. Add beetroot and half the chives to cabbage mixture; toss gently to combine.

4 Arrange radicchio on a serving platter; sprinkle with cabbage mixture. Crumble goat's cheese over salad; top with nuts and remaining chives. Drizzle with oil.

SWEET
Plates

LIME AND PASSIONFRUIT FROZEN YOGHURT CAKE

PREP + COOK TIME 1 HOUR 15 MINUTES (+ COOLING & FREEZING) SERVES 12

You will need to make this recipe the day before.

¾ cup (110g) plain (all-purpose) flour

¼ cup (35g) self-raising flour

½ teaspoon bicarbonate of soda (baking soda)

2 teaspoons finely grated lime rind

⅓ cup (90g) firmly packed grated palm sugar

60g (2 ounces) butter

⅓ cup (115g) golden syrup or treacle

1 egg

½ cup (125ml) buttermilk

1½ cups (420g) Greek-style yoghurt

300ml thickened (heavy) cream

⅔ cup (160ml) passionfruit pulp

CANDIED LIME

1½ cups (305g) firmly packed grated palm sugar

½ cup (125ml) water

2 tablespoons lime juice

1 stalk fresh lemon grass, quartered, bruised

4 limes, sliced thinly

1 Make candied lime.

2 Preheat oven to 170°C/340°F. Grease a 26cm x 32cm (10½-inch x 12¾-inch) swiss roll pan; line base and long sides with baking paper, extending the paper 5cm (2 inches) over the sides.

3 Sift flours and soda into a medium bowl; stir in rind.

Heat sugar, butter and golden syrup in a small pan over low heat until sugar dissolves; stir butter mixture, egg and buttermilk into flour mixture. Pour mixture into pan.

4 Bake for 12 minutes or until cake shrinks away from sides of pan slightly. Brush warm cake with 2 tablespoons of the reserved candied lime syrup. Cool in pan.

5 Line base and sides of a deep 14cm x 23cm (5½-inch x 9¼-inch) loaf pan with baking paper.

6 Beat yoghurt and cream in a small bowl with an electric mixer until soft peaks form; fold in all but 1 tablespoon of the remaining reserved candied lime syrup and half the passionfruit pulp. Pour one-third of yoghurt mixture into loaf pan. Trim a 12cm x 22cm (4¾-inch x 9-inch) piece from cake; carefully place in pan over yoghurt. Cover; freeze 1 hour or until firm. Refrigerate remaining yoghurt mixture. Cover remaining cake.

7 Pour remaining yoghurt mixture into pan. Trim a 14cm x 23cm (5½-inch x 9¼-inch) piece from remaining cake; carefully place in pan over yoghurt. Cover; freeze 3 hours or overnight.

8 Turn cake onto a platter; stand 10 minutes before serving. Top with candied lime. Combine remaining tablespoon of reserved candied lime syrup with remaining passionfruit pulp; drizzle over cake.

candied lime Stir sugar, the water, juice and lemon grass in a medium heavy-based saucepan over low heat until sugar dissolves. Bring to the boil. Reduce heat; simmer for 3 minutes or until syrup is reduced. Remove from heat; add lime, leave syrup to cool. Drain; reserve lime and syrup separately. Discard lemon grass.

YOU WILL NEED ABOUT 8 PASSIONFRUIT FOR THIS RECIPE. YOU CAN SUBSTITUTE CANNED PASSIONFRUIT PULP, IF YOU LIKE, HOWEVER TO COMPENSATE FOR THE SUGAR ADDED DURING CANNING ADD A TEASPOON OR TWO OF LIME JUICE.

PANNA COTTA AND COCONUT WAFERS
CAN BE MADE A DAY AHEAD.

COCONUT PANNA COTTA WITH MANGO AND COCONUT WAFERS

PREP + COOK TIME 45 MINUTES (+ COOLING & REFRIGERATION) **SERVES** 6

300ml pouring cream

½ cup (110g) caster (superfine) sugar

2 teaspoons powdered gelatine

⅓ cup (80ml) boiling water

375g (12 ounces) Greek-style vanilla yoghurt

1 teaspoon coconut extract

COCONUT WAFERS

1 sheet puff pastry

1 egg white

½ cup (40g) desiccated coconut

CARAMELISED MANGOES

2 medium mangoes (860g)

⅓ cup (75g) caster (superfine) sugar

CARAMEL SAUCE

⅓ cup (75g) caster (superfine) sugar

⅓ cup (80ml) water

2 tablespoons lemon juice

1 Stir cream and sugar in a medium saucepan, over high heat, without boiling, until sugar dissolves. Sprinkle gelatine over the boiling water in a small heatproof jug, stand jug in a small saucepan of simmering water; stir until gelatine dissolves. Stir gelatine mixture into hot cream mixture. Transfer to a medium bowl; cool.

2 Stir yoghurt and extract into cooled cream mixture.

3 Rinse six ½-cup (125ml) moulds with cold water; drain, do not wipe dry. Pour yoghurt mixture into moulds, cover loosely with plastic wrap. Refrigerate 4 hours or until set.

4 Make coconut wafers and caramelised mangoes, then caramel sauce.

5 Carefully turn panna cotta onto serving plates, add mangoes; spoon over the sauce. Serve with wafers.

coconut wafers Preheat oven to 200°C/400°F. Grease and line an oven tray with baking paper. Cut pastry in half, cut each half into four triangles; place on oven tray. Bake about 10 minutes. Remove from oven, brush with egg white, sprinkle with coconut. Bake a further 5 minutes or until coconut is golden.

caramelised mangoes Remove cheeks from mangoes; using a large metal spoon, scoop flesh from skin then cut in half lengthways. Sprinkle cut surfaces of mango with sugar. Heat a large frying pan; cook mango, cut-side down, 2 minutes or until caramelised. Remove from pan; cool.

caramel sauce Place sugar and 2 tablespoons of the water in a small heavy-based saucepan over medium heat; cook, swirling pan frequently, for 4 minutes or until deep golden. Add juice and the remaining water; swirl pan until combined and syrupy. Cool completely.

MIDDLE-EASTERN STYLE FRUIT SALAD

PREP + COOK TIME 30 MINUTES SERVES 8

4 medium navel oranges (960g)

10 cardamom pods

1 cup (220g) caster (superfine) sugar

2 cups (500ml) water

1 vanilla bean, split lengthways, seeds scraped

2 medium carrots (240g), cut into matchsticks

1 pomegranate (450g)

4 medium blood oranges (960g)

6 medium peaches (900g), halved, stones removed, cut into wedges

⅔ cup (160ml) freshly-squeezed orange juice

½ cup (125ml) freshly-squeezed lemon juice

1 Using a vegetable peeler, peel rind from one navel orange. Place rind in a small saucepan with cardamom, sugar, the water and vanilla seeds and bean; stir over low heat until sugar dissolves.

2 Add carrot to pan and increase heat to medium; cook for 20 minutes or until syrup is thick and carrot is translucent. Using a fork, transfer candied carrot to a small bowl. Transfer unstrained syrup to a large bowl.

3 Remove seeds from pomegranate; reserve seeds. Using a small sharp knife, remove rind and pith from navel and blood oranges, following the curve of the fruit. Cut oranges into 5mm (¼-inch) thick rounds; add to the syrup with pomegranate seeds and peaches. Add juices to bowl; stir to combine.

4 Stir half the candied carrot into fruit salad. Divide fruit salad among small bowls; serve topped with remaining candied carrot.

YOU WILL NEED ABOUT 3 EXTRA NAVEL ORANGES AND 2 LEMONS FOR THE JUICE IN THIS RECIPE.

TART CAN BE MADE A DAY AHEAD.

CANDIED BLOOD ORANGES ARE BEST MADE CLOSE TO SERVING.

TANGELO TART WITH CANDIED BLOOD ORANGES

PREP + COOK TIME 1 HOUR 50 MINUTES (+ REFRIGERATION, COOLING & STANDING) SERVES 8

1½ cups (225g) plain (all-purpose) flour

2 tablespoons icing (confectioners') sugar

125g (4 ounces) cold butter, chopped coarsely

1 egg yolk

1 tablespoon chilled water

1 tablespoon finely grated tangelo rind

½ cup (125ml) strained freshly squeezed tangelo juice

5 eggs

¾ cup (165g) caster (superfine) sugar

300ml pouring cream

CANDIED BLOOD ORANGES

½ cup (110g) caster (superfine) sugar

1½ cups (375ml) water

½ cup (125ml) strained freshly squeezed blood orange juice

3 medium blood oranges (480g), cut into 5mm (¼-inch) slices

½ cup (180g) honey

1 Process flour, icing sugar and butter until mixture resembles breadcrumbs. Add egg yolk and the chilled water; process until ingredients just come together. Wrap pastry in plastic wrap; refrigerate 30 minutes.

2 Grease a 3cm (1¼-inch) deep, 23cm (9¼-inch) round loose-based tart tin. Roll pastry between sheets of baking paper until 3mm (⅛-inch) thick and large enough to line the tin. Lift pastry into tin, ease into base and side, trim edge; prick base all over with a fork. Cover; refrigerate 20 minutes.

3 Meanwhile, preheat oven to 190°C/375°F.

4 Place tin on an oven tray; line pastry with baking paper, fill with dried beans or rice. Bake for 10 minutes. Remove paper and beans; bake a further 10 minutes or until browned lightly. Cool on tray.

5 Reduce oven temperature to 170°C/325°F.

6 Whisk rind, juice, eggs, caster sugar and cream in a large bowl until combined; strain into pastry case.

7 Bake tart for 35 minutes or until just set. Cool. Cover; refrigerate 3 hours or overnight.

8 Make candied blood oranges.

9 Stand tart at room temperature 30 minutes before serving; top with half the candied blood oranges and a little syrup. Serve tart cut into slices with remaining candied blood oranges and syrup.

candied blood oranges Stir sugar, the water and juice in a large frying pan over medium heat until sugar dissolves. Add orange; simmer for 20 minutes or until rind is soft. Add honey to pan; simmer a further 15 minutes or until oranges are candied and syrup is thickened.

PLUM AND GINGER CROSTATA

PREP + COOK TIME 1 HOUR 15 MINUTES (+ FREEZING & STANDING) **SERVES** 8

7 large yellow-fleshed black plums (1.2kg), cut into thin wedges

1 egg, beaten lightly

¼ cup (55g) demerara sugar

2 tablespoons glacé ginger, chopped

PASTRY

1⅔ cups (250g) plain (all-purpose) flour

⅓ cup (55g) icing (confectioners') sugar

½ teaspoon salt

150g (4½ ounces) cold unsalted butter, chopped finely

¼ cup (60ml) iced water

WALNUT AND GINGER PASTE

¾ cup (75g) walnuts, roasted

½ cup (115g) glacé ginger

50g (1½ ounces) soft butter

2 tablespoons instant polenta

1 tablespoon plain (all-purpose) flour

1 egg yolk

1 Make pastry.
2 Make walnut and ginger paste.

3 Preheat oven to 190°C/375°F.
4 Roll out pastry between two pieces of floured baking paper until 35cm (14-inch) round. Remove top piece of baking paper; carefully lift baking paper with pastry onto a large oven tray. Using a 26cm (10-inch) bowl or plate as a guide, mark a round in the centre of the pastry. Spread walnut and ginger paste in the marked round.
5 Starting at the edge of the filled round, place plum wedges in concentric circles. Carefully fold pastry edge in, pleating it as you go to partially cover the outside circle of plums. Brush folded edge with egg. Sprinkle sugar over plums and pastry.
6 Bake crostata for 40 minutes or until pastry is golden and filling cooked. Stand on tray 20 minutes. Just before serving, top with glacé ginger.

pastry Process flour, sugar and salt until combined. Add butter; process until mixture resembles breadcrumbs. Add the iced water; pulse until mixture almost comes together. Turn dough onto a work surface and form into a thin disc. Wrap in plastic wrap; freeze 30 minutes only.

walnut and ginger paste Process ingredients until mixture forms a smooth paste.

serving suggestion Serve with thick (double) cream or ice-cream.

IF YOU DON'T PLAN TO USE THE PASTRY AFTER 30 MINUTES, PLACE IT IN THE REFRIGERATOR FOR AT LEAST 1 HOUR OR UP TO A DAY.

TRY ROASTED FIGS, PEARS AND PLUMS OR FRESH RASPBERRIES, BLACKBERRIES AND STRAWBERRIES INSTEAD OF PEACHES.

RICOTTA CAKES WITH HONEY AND ROASTED PEACHES

PREP + COOK TIME 50 MINUTES (+ REFRIGERATION) MAKES 4

You will need a 50cm (20-inch) square of muslin available from kitchen and fabric supply stores.

200g (6 ounces) unsalted butter, softened

1 cup (220g) caster (superfine) sugar

1.5kg (3 pounds) firm ricotta

1 cup (240g) crème fraîche

6 small peaches (690g), halved, stones removed

2 tablespoons brown sugar

½ cup (115g) honey

¼ cup (35g) pistachios, halved

125g (4 ounces) loaf brioche, sliced, toasted

1 Cut four 25cm (10-inch) squares of muslin then cut out a hole from the centre of each square. Line four 10cm (4-inch) bundt pans (1-cup capacity) each with a muslin square.

2 Beat butter and caster sugar in a small bowl with an electric mixer until light and fluffy. Add ricotta, beat until combined; fold in crème fraîche. Spoon mixture into pans; using wet fingers, press down very firmly on the surface to compact the mixture in the pan. Cover; refrigerate 2 hours or until firm.

3 Preheat oven to 180°C/350°F.

4 Grease and line an oven tray with baking paper. Place peaches, cut-side up, on tray; sprinkle with brown sugar. Roast for 20 minutes or until caramelised. Peel away peach skins.

5 Invert ricotta cakes onto serving plates; carefully peel away muslin. Drizzle ricotta cakes with honey; top with pistachios. Serve with warm or cooled peaches and toasted brioche.

tip Ricotta cakes can be made up to 2 days ahead. If peach stones are difficult to remove, leave them in during roasting – they will come out more easily after cooking.

PISTACHIO, WALNUT AND CHOCOLATE BAKLAVA

PREP + COOK TIME 1 HOUR 10 MINUTES (+ COOLING & STANDING) MAKES 36

12 sheets fillo pastry

125g (4 ounces) butter, melted

2 tablespoons finely chopped walnuts

FILLING

1½ cups (210g) pistachios

2 cups (200g) walnuts

200g (6 ounces) dark (semi-sweet) chocolate, chopped coarsely

⅓ cup (75g) caster (superfine) sugar

2 teaspoons ground cinnamon

1½ tablespoons finely grated orange rind

HONEY SYRUP

1½ cups (330g) caster (superfine) sugar

1½ cups (375ml) water

½ cup (175g) honey

1 medium orange (240g), rind peeled in long strips

⅓ cup (80ml) orange juice

1 Preheat oven to 190°C/375°F. Grease a 22cm x 40cm x 2.5cm (9-inch x 16-inch x 1-inch) oven tray, then line with baking paper.

2 Make filling.

3 Layer three pastry sheets, brushing each with a little of the butter. Spread one-quarter of the filling over pastry, leaving a 3cm (1¼-inch) border along both long sides. Starting at one long side, roll up pastry to form a log. Place log on oven tray, brush with butter. Repeat with remaining pastry, butter and filling.

4 Bake baklava for 20 minutes or until golden.

5 Meanwhile, make honey syrup.

6 Stand baklava in tray 5 minutes to cool slightly. Using a small sharp knife, cut each log diagonally into nine 2cm (¾-inch) wide pieces. Pour hot syrup over baklava; stand in the tray 3 hours or until syrup is absorbed. Serve topped with chopped walnuts.

filling Place nuts on an oven tray; roast in oven for 5 minutes or until browned lightly. Cool completely. Process nuts with remaining ingredients until finely chopped.

honey syrup Stir sugar, the water, honey and rind in a small saucepan, over medium heat, without boiling, until sugar dissolves. Bring to a simmer. Simmer for 20 minutes or until thickened slightly. Stir in juice.

tip To prevent the fillo pastry from drying out while you're not using it, keep it covered with a layer of plastic wrap and a damp tea towel.

serving suggestion Serve with Greek-style yoghurt.

LINING THE CAKE PAN WITH A LAYER OF FOIL WILL KEEP IT 'WATER TIGHT' DURING COOKING.

BERRY AND TAMARILLO CROISSANT PUDDING CAKE

PREP + COOK TIME 2 HOURS 15 MINUTES (+ REFRIGERATION, COOLING & STANDING) SERVES 12

8 croissants (400g), each torn into 4 pieces

125g (4 ounces) raspberries

600ml pouring cream

1 cup (250ml) milk

⅔ cup (150g) caster (superfine) sugar

8 eggs

1 teaspoon vanilla bean paste

2 tablespoons demerara sugar

BERRY AND TAMARILLO JAM

5 tamarillos (660g)

250g (8 ounces) strawberries, halved (quartered if large)

1 cup (220g) caster (superfine) sugar

1 tablespoon finely grated tangelo rind

½ teaspoon vanilla bean paste

1 star anise

1 Make berry and tamarillo jam.
2 Preheat oven to 160°C/325°F. Line base and side of a 24cm (9½-inch) springform pan with one piece of extra wide foil, taking care not to tear foil. Line base only with baking paper; grease whole pan well.
3 Place croissant pieces, torn-side up, in pan; spoon three-quarters of the jam over croissants. Cut reserved tamarillos into thin wedges; place two-thirds of the slices between croissant pieces. Top with raspberries.
4 Add remaining tamarillo wedges to jam; stir to combine. Refrigerate until needed.
5 Whisk cream, milk, caster sugar, eggs and paste in a large bowl until combined. Slowly pour custard over croissant and fruit; gently shake pan to ensure custard is evenly distributed.
6 Place pan on an oven tray; bake for 1½ hours or until golden and just set (custard should still wobble as it will set further on standing). Sprinkle with demerara sugar; stand in pan 30 minutes. Serve pudding cake warm or at room temperature, topped with remaining jam and, if you like, whipped cream.

berry and tamarillo jam Score skin at the base of each tamarillo with a sharp knife; plunge into boiling water briefly then into iced water. Remove skin; reserve 3 tamarillos for pudding. Chop each remaining tamarillo into 12 pieces; place in a small heavy-based saucepan. Add strawberries, sugar, rind, paste and star anise; cook, covered, over low heat, shaking pan occasionally about 5 minutes. Simmer, uncovered, a further 15 minutes or until mixture thickens. Strain mixture through a fine sieve over a heatproof bowl. Return syrup to pan; simmer over medium heat until reduced by half. Combine reduced syrup with fruit; cool.

do-ahead Jam can be made a day ahead. Store in an airtight container in the fridge. Pudding is best made on the day.

PISTACHIO AND LEMON CURD CAKE

PREP + COOK TIME 1 HOUR 20 MINUTES (+ REFRIGERATION) **SERVES** 12

cooking-oil spray

1¼ cups (160g) finely chopped pistachios

125g (4 ounces) unsalted butter

1 cup (220g) caster (superfine) sugar

1 tablespoon finely grated lemon rind

3 eggs

⅔ cup (100g) cake flour

1 teaspoon baking powder

LEMON CURD

3 eggs

1½ tablespoons finely grated lemon rind

½ cup (125ml) lemon juice

¾ cup (165g) caster (superfine) sugar

100g (3½ ounces) unsalted butter

1 Make lemon curd.
2 Preheat oven to 180°C/350°F. Grease a 22cm (9-inch) springform pan; line base and side with two layers of baking paper. Spray the sides with oil, avoiding the base. Place ¼ cup of the nuts in the pan; rotate pan on its side to coat side with nuts.
3 Beat butter, sugar and rind in a medium bowl with an electric mixer about 3 minutes until pale and fluffy. Beat in eggs, one at a time, until combined.
4 Sift flour and baking powder into a small bowl, add ⅔ cup of the nuts; stir to combine. Using a large metal spoon, fold dry ingredients into the egg mixture until just combined.
5 Spoon cake mixture into pan; drop pan on work surface to settle the mixture. Spread 1 cup of the curd over batter, levelling the surface; scatter evenly with remaining pistachios. Cover remaining curd; refrigerate.
6 Bake about 40 minutes; cover surface with a round of baking paper to prevent nuts burning, then bake a further 10 minutes or until a skewer inserted into the centre comes out clean (the top will still be slightly wobbly). Serve cake warm or at room temperature with remaining lemon curd.

lemon curd Combine eggs, rind, juice and sugar in a medium heatproof bowl set over a medium saucepan of simmering water. Stir for 10 minutes or until mixture thickens and thickly coats the back of a spoon. Gradually add butter, stirring until smooth between additions. Strain mixture into a medium bowl. Cover surface with plastic wrap; cool. Refrigerate 3 hours or until chilled.

tips You can finely chop the pistachios in a food processor if you like; use the pulse button, in bursts, for an even texture. If you can't find cake flour, substitute with ½ cup plain flour and 2 tablespoons cornflour. It is best to use freshly squeezed lemon juice in the lemon curd.

LEMON CURD CAN BE MADE UP TO 1 WEEK AHEAD;

STORE IN AN AIRTIGHT CONTAINER IN THE REFRIGERATOR.

CAKE IS BEST MADE ON THE DAY OF SERVING.

TO CHECK THAT YOU HAVE BEATEN THE MERINGUE
SUFFICIENTLY, RUB A LITTLE OF THE MIXTURE
BETWEEN YOUR FINGERS – IT SHOULD FEEL SILKY
SMOOTH, WITHOUT ANY GRAINY SUGAR CRYSTALS.

CHOCOLATE CHERRY BERRY PAVLOVA

PREP + COOK TIME 2 HOURS (+ COOLING) **SERVES** 10

100g (3 ounces) dark (semi-sweet) chocolate, chopped

4 egg whites

1 cup (220g) caster (superfine) sugar

1 tablespoon cornflour (cornstarch)

1 teaspoon white vinegar

250g (8 ounces) cream cheese, softened

2 teaspoons vanilla extract

¼ cup (40g) icing (confectioners') sugar

300ml thickened (heavy) cream

fresh cherries with stems attached

CHERRY BLUEBERRY COMPOTE

2 cups (300g) cherries, halved, pitted

1 cup (150g) blueberries

⅓ cup (75g) caster (superfine) sugar

¼ cup (60ml) water

¼ cup (80g) cherry jam

1 Preheat oven to 120°C/250°F. Line an oven tray with baking paper. Mark an 18cm (7¼-inch) circle on paper.

2 Place chocolate in a small heatproof bowl over a small saucepan of simmering water (don't allow bowl to touch water); stir until just melted. Cool slightly.

3 Beat egg whites in a small bowl with an electric mixer until soft peaks form; gradually add caster sugar, beating until dissolved after each addition and mixture is thick and glossy.

4 Fold cornflour and vinegar into meringue mixture; swirl in chocolate. Dollop meringue inside marked circle on tray.

5 Bake for 1¼ hours or until dry to the touch. Turn oven off, leave meringue to cool in oven with door ajar.

6 Meanwhile, make cherry blueberry compote.

7 Beat cream cheese, extract and icing sugar in a small bowl with an electric mixer until smooth; gradually beat in cream until smooth and combined.

8 Just before serving, spoon cream cheese mixture on pavlova; top with compote. Decorate with fresh cherries.

cherry blueberry compote Place cherries, blueberries, sugar and the water in a medium saucepan over medium heat; bring to a simmer. Simmer for 5 minutes or until cherries and blueberries have released juices. Using a slotted spoon, transfer cherries and blueberries to a small bowl. Stir jam into juices in pan; bring to the boil. Boil for 5 minutes or until mixture thickens. Pour syrup over cherry mixture. Cool completely.

do-ahead Meringue can be made a day ahead; store in an airtight container at room temperature. Topping is best made close to serving.

MOCHA MERINGUE STACK

PREP + COOK TIME 1 HOUR 45 MINUTES (+ COOLING) SERVES 12

1 tablespoon instant coffee granules

1 teaspoon boiling water

8 egg whites

1 teaspoon cream of tartar

2 cups (440g) raw caster (superfine) sugar

1 tablespoon cornflour (cornstarch)

2 teaspoons white vinegar

2 teaspoons icing (confectioners') sugar

CHOCOLATE SAUCE

180g (5½ ounces) dark (semi-sweet) chocolate, chopped

30g (1 ounce) unsalted butter, chopped

1 cup (250ml) thickened (heavy) cream

¼ cup (40g) icing (confectioners') sugar

COFFEE CREAM

1 tablespoon instant coffee granules

2 teaspoons boiling water

300ml thickened (heavy) cream

¼ cup (40g) icing (confectioners') sugar

2 tablespoons coffee-flavoured liqueur

300ml thick (double) cream

1 Preheat oven to 120°C/250°F. Line three large oven trays with baking paper.
2 Stir coffee and the water in a small bowl until dissolved. Beat egg whites and cream of tartar in a large bowl with an electric mixer until soft peaks form. Gradually add caster sugar, beating until dissolved between additions. Beat in cornflour, vinegar and coffee mixture on low speed until just combined (overbeating at this stage will cause the meringue to deflate).
3 Drop ¼-cups of meringue mixture onto trays 5cm (2-inches) apart; you should get about 24 meringues. Bake for 1 hour or until dry to touch. Turn oven off, leave meringues to cool in oven with door ajar.
4 Make chocolate sauce, then coffee cream.
5 Spoon a little coffee cream onto a platter, arrange nine of the meringues on top. Spread the base of each remaining meringue with 2 tablespoons of coffee cream, stacking them into a pyramid shape. Drizzle stack with half the chocolate sauce, then dust with icing sugar. Serve stack immediately with remaining coffee cream and sauce.

chocolate sauce Stir chocolate, butter and cream in a medium saucepan over low heat until just melted. Remove from heat; gradually whisk in sifted icing sugar. Cool to room temperature (about 20 minutes) until thickened.

coffee cream Stir coffee and the water in a small bowl until dissolved; refrigerate 5 minutes. Beat thickened cream, sugar, liqueur and coffee mixture in a small bowl with an electric mixer until soft peaks form. Add thick cream; beat until soft peaks form.

do-ahead Meringues can be made 2 days ahead; store in an airtight container at room temperature. Chocolate sauce can be made several hours ahead; reheat until just warm before serving. Assemble meringue stack close to serving.

MERINGUES COULD TAKE UP TO 1 ½ HOURS
TO COOK, DEPENDING ON THE SIZE OF YOUR OVEN.
IF YOU DON'T HAVE ENOUGH SPACE OR SHELVES IN
YOUR OVEN, MAKE MERINGUES IN BATCHES.

CAKE AND CANDIED BEETROOT CAN BOTH
BE MADE A DAY AHEAD. STORE SEPARATELY IN
AIRTIGHT CONTAINERS IN THE REFRIGERATOR.

FLOURLESS CHOCOLATE BEETROOT CAKE

PREP + COOK TIME 2 HOURS (+ REFRIGERATION & COOLING) **SERVES** 12

300g (9½ ounces) beetroot (beets), peeled, cut in 3cm (1¼-inch) pieces

350g (11 ounces) dark (semi-sweet) chocolate, chopped

185g (6 ounces) butter, chopped

6 eggs

1 teaspoon vanilla extract

1 cup (220g) firmly packed brown sugar

1 cup (100g) ground hazelnuts

1 teaspoon dutch-processed cocoa

CANDIED BEETROOT

1½ cups (330g) caster (superfine) sugar

1 cup (250ml) water

2 small beetroot (beets) (200g), peeled, sliced thinly

1 tablespoon lemon juice

SWEETENED CRÈME FRAÎCHE

1½ cups (360g) crème fraîche

2 tablespoons icing (confectioners') sugar, sifted

1 teaspoon vanilla extract

1 Cook beetroot in a small saucepan of boiling water for 45 minutes or until tender. Drain, reserving 2 tablespoons of the cooking liquid. Process beetroot and reserved liquid until smooth. You should have 1 cup beetroot puree.

2 Preheat oven to 160°C/325°F. Grease a 22cm (9-inch) springform pan; line base and side with baking paper.

3 Stir chocolate and butter in a small saucepan over low heat until melted and smooth.

4 Whisk eggs, extract, sugar and ground hazelnuts in a large bowl until combined. Add chocolate mixture and beetroot puree; whisk to combine. Pour mixture into pan; cover with foil.

5 Bake for 1 hour 10 minutes or until cooked around the edge with a slight wobble in the centre. Lift up edge of foil to release steam. Refrigerate cake for at least 3 hours or overnight.

6 Make candied beetroot, then sweetened crème fraîche.

7 Place cake on a platter; dust edges with cocoa. Spread top of cake with sweetened crème fraîche. Top with candied beetroot and drizzle with reserved syrup.

candied beetroot Stir sugar and the water in a small saucepan over medium heat until sugar dissolves. Bring to the boil. Add beetroot; cook for 20 minutes or until beetroot slices become slightly translucent and syrup thickens. Using two forks, transfer beetroot from syrup to a baking-paper-lined oven tray to cool. Reserve 1 cup of the syrup; stir in juice.

sweetened crème fraîche Whisk ingredients together in a small bowl until soft peaks form.

tip Use a mandoline or V-slicer to slice the beetroot into thin rounds for candying.

PEACH AND NECTARINE TART

PREP + COOK TIME 55 MINUTES SERVES 8

60g (2 ounces) butter, softened

⅓ cup (75g) caster (superfine) sugar

1 egg

½ teaspoon orange blossom water

¾ cup (75g) ground almonds

2 tablespoons plain (all-purpose) flour

2 x 375g (12-ounce) packets puff pastry

4 large peaches (880g)

1 nectarine (170g)

150g (4½ ounces) raspberries

¼ cup (35g) coarsely chopped pistachios

¼ cup (90g) honey

1 Beat butter and sugar in a small bowl with an electric mixer until creamy. Beat in egg and orange blossom water until combined. Stir in ground almonds and flour.
2 Preheat oven to 220°C/425°F.
3 Roll out each packet of pastry on a floured sheet of baking paper into a 16cm x 34cm (6½-inch x 13½-inch) rectangle. Lift each pastry rectangle onto an oven tray. Spread almond mixture thinly over pastry, leaving a 1cm (½-inch) border.
4 Cut peaches and nectarine in half; remove stones. Cut halves into thin wedges. Arrange fruit wedges, overlapping slightly, on almond mixture.
5 Bake for 30 minutes or until browned and pastry is cooked underneath. Serve tarts topped with raspberries and pistachios; drizzle with honey.

serving suggestion Serve warm or cool with thick (double) cream or ice-cream.

WE USED A LOAF PAN WITH A CAPACITY OF
2.2 LITRES (9 CUPS). TO LINE THE PAN SMOOTHLY
WITH PLASTIC WRAP, DAMPEN IT FIRST.

POACHED PEAR, MASCARPONE AND DESSERT WINE CAKE

PREP + COOK TIME 50 MINUTES (+ COOLING & REFRIGERATION) SERVES 8

You will need to make this recipe the day before.

6 medium beurre bosc pears (1.4kg)

1 vanilla bean

3½ cups (770g) caster (superfine) sugar

3 cups (750ml) sweet white wine

2 cups (500ml) water

500g (1 pound) mascarpone

¾ cup (180ml) thickened (heavy) cream

2 egg yolks

1 tablespoon icing (confectioners') sugar

60g (2 ounces) dark (semi-sweet) chocolate, grated

2 tablespoons brandy

375g (12 ounces) sponge finger biscuits

1 Peel pears, leaving stalks intact, then halve. Split vanilla bean in half lengthways; scrape seeds. Add seeds and bean to a large saucepan with caster sugar, wine and the water; stir over medium heat until sugar dissolves. Bring to the boil. Reduce heat; simmer about 1 minute. Add pears; cover pears with a round of baking paper and a small plate to keep pears submerged. Simmer for 15 minutes or until pears are tender. Cool.

2 Beat mascarpone, cream, egg yolks and icing sugar in a large bowl with an electric mixer until soft peaks form. Fold in grated chocolate. Cover; refrigerate until needed.

3 Line a 7.5cm (3-inch) deep, 10cm x 23cm (4-inch x 9¼-inch) loaf pan with plastic wrap, extending wrap over the sides.

4 Cut 2 pear halves into 1cm (½-inch) slices. Combine 2 cups (500ml) of the pear poaching liquid with brandy in a large bowl. Dip both sides of 8 or 9 biscuits, one at a time, into poaching liquid; place biscuits crossways into base of pan, trimming to fit if necessary. Spread 1½ cups (375ml) mascarpone mixture over biscuits; top with sliced pears, overlapping slightly. Spread a 5mm (¼-inch) layer of mascarpone mixture over pear layer. Dip 10 biscuits into poaching liquid; place lengthways on mascarpone layer, trimming to fit if necessary. Spread remaining mascarpone mixture over biscuits; finish layering with another 10 dipped biscuits. Tap pan lightly on work surface to settle the mixture. Cover with plastic wrap; refrigerate overnight.

5 Meanwhile, simmer 1 cup (250ml) of the poaching liquid and the vanilla bean in a small saucepan over medium heat for 5 minutes or until thickened. Cool; refrigerate until needed.

6 To serve, turn cake out of pan onto a platter; remove plastic wrap. Place half the pears and vanilla bean on top of cake; drizzle with thickened syrup. Serve cake with remaining pears.

tips We used moscato, a low alcohol, lightly sparkling Italian wine. When serving, you could cut the pears into quarters if you prefer.

PANETTONE CUSTARD PUDDING WITH MACERATED FRUIT

PREP + COOK TIME 1 HOUR 45 MINUTES **SERVES** 8

½ x 500g (1 pound) panettone

90g (3 ounces) soft butter

3 cups (750ml) milk

300ml thickened (heavy) cream

½ cup (110g) caster (superfine) sugar

1 teaspoon finely grated orange rind

4cm (1½-inch) piece vanilla bean, split lengthways

4 eggs

2 egg yolks

1 tablespoon apricot jam

1 tablespoon orange-flavoured liqueur

MACERATED FRUIT

200g (6½ ounces) raspberries

250g (8 ounces) strawberries, halved

200g (6½ ounces) blueberries

1 medium mango (430g), chopped

2 tablespoons caster (superfine) sugar

¼ cup (60ml) orange-flavoured liqueur

SOURED CREAM

½ cup (125ml) thickened (heavy) cream

⅓ cup (80g) sour cream

1 tablespoons icing (confectioners') sugar

1 Preheat grill (broiler).

2 Cut panettone into 1cm (½-inch) slices. Place under grill until lightly toasted on both sides. While panettone is hot, spread with butter, then cut into fingers. Place fingers in a criss-cross pattern in a shallow 1.5-litre (6-cup) ovenproof dish.

3 Stir milk, cream, sugar, rind and vanilla bean in a saucepan, over medium heat, until sugar dissolves; bring almost to the boil. Remove from heat. Cover; stand 10 minutes. Strain mixture through a sieve into a heatproof jug.

4 Preheat oven to 180°C/350°F.

5 Whisk eggs and egg yolks in a medium bowl; gradually whisk in milk mixture. Pour custard over panettone. Place dish in a large baking dish; add enough boiling water to the baking dish to come halfway up the sides of the ovenproof dish.

6 Bake for 1 hour or until browned lightly and set. Remove pudding dish from baking dish.

7 Meanwhile, make macerated fruit, then make soured cream.

8 Brush hot pudding with combined jam and liqueur; serve warm or cold with fruit and soured cream.

macerated fruit Combine ingredients in a large bowl.

soured cream Beat thickened cream in a small bowl with an electric mixer until soft peaks form. Add sour cream and sifted sugar, beat briefly until soft peaks form again.

PANETTONE ARE EASY TO FIND AROUND CHRISTMAS TIME, AT OTHER TIMES THEY MAY NOT BE AS READILY AVAILABLE. YOU CAN USE BRIOCHE INSTEAD, ADDING A HANDFUL OF SULTANAS, OR THICK-CUT FRUIT BREAD.

AS THE PASTRY IS VERY SHORT,
IT'S IMPORTANT TO REFRIGERATE
IT BETWEEN STEPS SO IT'S
EASIER TO HANDLE.

MANGO AND MACADAMIA TART

PREP + COOK TIME 1 HOUR 30 MINUTES (+ REFRIGERATION & COOLING) SERVES 10

¼ cup (35g) macadamias

1⅓ cups (200g) plain (all-purpose) flour

1 tablespoon caster (superfine) sugar

100g (3 ounces) cold butter, chopped coarsely

2 tablespoons iced water, approximately

2 medium mangoes (860g), sliced thinly

FILLING

2 teaspoons powdered gelatine

2 tablespoons water

1¼ cups (310ml) thickened (heavy) cream

250g (8 ounces) cream cheese, softened

½ cup (110g) caster (superfine) sugar

1 tablespoon lime juice

LIME SYRUP

1 cup (220g) caster (superfine) sugar

½ cup (125ml) water

1 teaspoon finely grated lime rind

2 tablespoons lime juice

1 Process macadamias until ground to fine breadcrumbs.
2 Combine flour, ground macadamias, sugar and a little salt in a large bowl; using fingertips, rub in butter until mixture resembles coarse breadcrumbs. Make a well in centre, add the iced water; mix until dough starts to come together. Knead dough on a lightly floured surface into a ball, flatten slightly. Wrap dough in plastic; refrigerate 20 minutes.
3 Grease an 11cm x 35cm (4-inch x 14-inch) loose-based rectangular fluted flan pan. Roll pastry between two sheets of baking paper until large enough to line pan; refrigerate 10 minutes. Lift pastry into pan, ease into base and sides; trim edge. Prick pastry base with fork; refrigerate 20 minutes.
4 Preheat oven to 200°C/400°F.
5 Line pastry with baking paper; fill with dried beans or rice. Bake about 15 minutes; remove paper and beans. Bake a further 20 minutes or until pastry is browned lightly. Cool.
6 Meanwhile, make filling.
7 Spread filling into tart shell. Refrigerate 4 hours or until set.
8 Make lime syrup.
9 Position overlapping mango slices on tart; drizzle with syrup.

filling Sprinkle gelatine over the water in a small heatproof jug; stand jug in a small saucepan of simmering water. Stir until gelatine dissolves. Cool 5 minutes. Beat cream in a small bowl with an electric mixer until soft peaks form. Beat cream cheese, sugar and juice in another small bowl with electric mixer until smooth. Stir in gelatine mixture; fold in cream.

lime syrup Stir sugar and the water in a small saucepan over high heat, without boiling, until sugar is dissolved. Bring to the boil. Reduce heat; simmer about 5 minutes. Remove from heat; stir in rind and juice.

MENUS

Cocktail party for a crowd

SERVES 60

This selection of bites is perfect for any stand-up event such as birthday gatherings or engagement parties.

Chorizo and potato fritters (page 11)
Fish scrolls with capsicum salsa (page 12)
Haloumi and avocado bruschetta (page 20)
Fried buttermilk and mustard chicken wings (page 27)
Chimichurri lamb cutlets (page 35)
Five spice squid with lime mayonnaise (page 43)
Middle-eastern salad cups (page 52)
Pistachio, walnut and chocolate baklava (page 158)

Casual lunch for girlfriends

SERVES 8

Try this menu next weekend when you invite the girls over for an informal get together. A light fresh menu suited for a long lazy lunch catching up with friends.

Baked ricotta with char-grilled vegetables (page 44)
Barbecued salmon with salsa criolla (page 97)
Lettuce wedges with creamy lemon dressing (page 115)
Tomato salad with labne and seeds (page 119)
Chocolate cherry pavlova (page 165)

Family gathering

SERVES 8

When the family comes together these dishes are
perfect for an informal buffet-style setting.

Roast pumpkin and fetta bruschetta (page 32)
Zucchini tarts (page 47)
Lime leaf chicken (page 61)
Prosciutto and pea tart (page 110)
Roasted asparagus and smashed potatoes (page 139)
Red salad (page 143)
Plum and ginger crostata (page 154)

Asian-inspired

SERVES 8

For a large gathering this menu will tantalise
the taste buds and have your guests talking for weeks.

Spiced tofu bao (page 77)
Chinese roast duck with green onion pancakes (page 78)
Coconut and prawn fritters with asian salad (page 93)
Gai lan with oyster sauce (page 127)
Lime and passionfruit frozen yoghurt cake (page 146)

Summer by the pool

SERVES 6

Warm summer days by the pool, cold beverage
in one hand and barbecue tongs in the other,
this menu is a pleaser for outdoor entertaining.

Smoked ocean trout and
pickled fennel buns (page 15)
Barbecued steaks with corn salad (page 101)
Middle-eastern style fruit salad (page 150)

Vegetarian feast

SERVES 8

Celebrate the magic of a warm relaxing afternoon
in the garden with a selection of vegetarian fare.

Zucchini tarts (page 47)
Mushroom sliders with
harissa crème fraiche (page 82)
Baby beetroot, lentil and watercress salad (page 132)
Pistachio and lemon curd cake (page 162)

Comfort food

SERVES 8

As the colder weather approaches,
this menu will leave your guests warm and cosy.

Ratatouille soup with pistou (page 48)
Tomato braised lamb shanks with
creamy polenta (page 62)
Warm beetroot and heirloom carrot salad (page 123)
Panettone custard pudding
with macerated fruit (page 174)

Sunday brunch

SERVES 6-8

This menu is suited for light mid-morning entertaining.

Ricotta and basil pancakes
with roasted tomatoes (page 16)
Chorizo, chickpea and pumpkin salad (page 105)
Peach and nectarine tart (page 170)

GLOSSARY

ALLSPICE also known as pimento or jamaican pepper; named because it tastes like a combination of nutmeg, cumin, clove and cinnamon. Available whole (a dark-brown berry the size of a pea) or ground.

ALMONDS
flaked paper-thin slices.
ground also called almond meal; almonds are powdered to a coarse flour-like texture.

BAKING POWDER a raising agent consisting mainly of two parts cream of tartar to one part bicarbonate of soda (baking soda).

BAY LEAVES aromatic leaves from the bay tree available fresh or dried; adds a strong, slightly peppery flavour.

BEANS
broad (fava) also called windsor and horse beans; available dried, fresh, canned and frozen. Fresh should be peeled twice (discarding both the outer long green pod and the beige-green tough inner skin); frozen beans have had their pods removed but the beige skin still needs removal.
green also known as french or string beans (although the tough string they once had has generally been bred out of them), this long thin fresh bean is consumed in its entirety once cooked.

BEETROOT (BEETS) also known as red beets; firm, round root vegetable.

BICARBONATE OF SODA (BAKING SODA) a raising agent.

BREAD
brioche French in origin; a rich, yeast-leavened, cake-like bread made with butter and eggs. Available from cake or specialty bread shops.
pitta also known as lebanese bread. This wheat-flour pocket bread is sold in large, flat pieces that separate into two thin rounds.
tortilla thin, round unleavened bread; can be purchased frozen, fresh or vacuum-packed. Two kinds are available, one made from wheat flour and the other from corn.

BUK CHOY also called bok choy, pak choi, chinese white cabbage or chinese chard; has a fresh, mild mustard taste.

BUTTERMILK originally the term given to the slightly sour liquid left after butter was churned from cream, today it is made from no-fat or low-fat milk to which specific bacterial cultures have been added. Despite its name, it is actually low in fat.

CAPERS grey-green buds of a warm climate (usually Mediterranean) shrub, sold either dried and salted or pickled in a vinegar brine. Capers must be rinsed well to wash away some of the brine before using.

CAPSICUM (BELL PEPPER) available in many colours: red, green, yellow, orange and purplish-black. Be sure to discard seeds and membranes before use.

CARDAMOM a spice native to India and used extensively in its cuisine; sold in pod, seed or ground form. Has a distinctive aromatic and sweetly rich flavour.

CAYENNE PEPPER dried, long, thin-fleshed, extremely hot, ground red chilli.

CHEESE
cheddar the most common cow's milk 'tasty' cheese; should be aged, hard and have a pronounced bite.
cream commonly called philadelphia or philly; a soft cow-milk cheese,
fetta Greek in origin; a crumbly textured goat- or sheep-milk cheese with a sharp, salty taste. It is ripened and stored in salted whey.
fetta, persian a soft, creamy cheese marinated in a blend of olive oil, garlic, herbs and spices.
goat's made from goat's milk, has an earthy, strong taste. Available in soft, crumbly and firm textures, and sometimes rolled in ash or herbs.
haloumi a Greek Cypriot cheese with a semi-firm, spongy texture and very salty sweet flavour. Ripened and stored in salted whey; best grilled or fried, it holds its shape well on being heated. Eat while still warm as it becomes tough and rubbery on cooling.
mascarpone a soft, creamy and spreadable fresh cultured-cream product made in much the same way as yoghurt. Whiteish to creamy yellow in colour, with a buttery-rich, luscious texture.

mozzarella soft, spun-curd cheese; originating in southern Italy where it was traditionally made from water-buffalo milk.

parmesan also called parmigiano; a hard, grainy cow-milk cheese originating in Italy.

pecorino the Italian generic name for the family of hard, white to pale-yellow cheeses made from sheep's milk.

ricotta a soft, sweet, moist, white cow-milk cheese with a low fat content and a slightly grainy texture.

CHICKPEAS (GARBANZO BEANS) also known as hummus or channa; an irregularly round, sandy-coloured legume. Firm texture even after cooking, a floury mouth-feel and robust nutty flavour; available canned or dried (reconstitute for several hours in cold water before use).

CHILLI
chipotle the name used for jalapeño chillies once they've been dried and smoked. Chipotles are dark brown, almost black, and wrinkled in appearance with a deep, intensely smoky flavour.

flakes dried, deep-red, dehydrated chilli slices and whole seeds.

green any unripened chilli; also some particular varieties that are ripe when green, such as jalapeño, habanero, poblano or serrano.

jalapeño fairly hot, medium-sized, plump, dark green chilli; available pickled, sold canned or bottled, and fresh, from greengrocers.

long red available both fresh and dried; a generic term used for any moderately hot, thin, long chilli.

powder can be used as a substitute for fresh chillies (½ teaspoon ground chilli powder to 1 chopped medium fresh chilli).

CHINESE FIVE-SPICE a fragrant mixture of ground cinnamon, cloves, star anise, sichuan pepper and fennel seeds. Used in Chinese and other Asian cooking; available from most supermarkets or Asian food shops.

CHOCOLATE, DARK (SEMI-SWEET) also called luxury chocolate; made of a high percentage of cocoa liquor and cocoa butter, and little added sugar.

CHORIZO SAUSAGES made from coarsely minced (ground) smoked pork and highly seasoned with garlic, chilli powder and other spices.

CINNAMON available in pieces (called sticks or quills) and ground into powder.

COCOA POWDER, DUTCH-PROCESSED treated with an alkali to neutralise its acids. It has a reddish-brown colour, a mild flavour and is easy to dissolve.

COCONUT
cream obtained commercially from the first pressing of the coconut flesh, without the addition of water.

desiccated concentrated, unsweetened, dried and finely shredded coconut flesh.

flakes dried flaked coconut flesh.

milk not the liquid found inside the fruit (coconut water) but the diluted liquid from the second pressing of the white flesh of a mature coconut.

CORNFLOUR (CORNSTARCH) used as a thickening agent in cooking; available made from corn or wheat.

CREAM
pouring also called pure or fresh cream. It contains no additives and has a minimum fat content of 35%.

thick (double) a dolloping cream with a minimum fat content of 45%.

thickened (heavy) a whipping cream that contains a thickener. It has a minimum fat content of 35%.

CREAM OF TARTAR the acid ingredient in baking powder; added to confectionery mixtures to help prevent sugar from crystallising. Keeps frostings creamy and improves volume when beating egg whites.

CRÈME FRAÎCHE a mature, naturally fermented cream with a minimum fat content of 35%. It has a velvety texture and slightly tangy, nutty flavour.

CUMIN also known as zeera or comino; has a spicy, almost curry-like flavour. Available dried as seeds or ground.

DAIKON also called white radish; this long, white horseradish has a sweet flavour. The flesh is white but the skin can be either white or black; buy those that are firm and unwrinkled from Asian food shops.

DUCK whole ducks are available from specialty chicken shops, open-air markets and some supermarkets.

EGGPLANT also called aubergine. Ranging in size from tiny to very large and in colour from pale green to deep purple. Can also be purchased char-grilled, packed in oil, in jars.

FENNEL also called finocchio or anise; a crunchy green vegetable slightly resembling celery that's eaten raw in salads, fried as an accompaniment or used as an ingredient in soups, sauces and many other dishes.

FISH SAUCE called naam pla on the label if Thai-made or nuoc naam if Vietnamese; the two are almost identical. Made from pulverised salted fermented fish (most often anchovies); has a pungent smell and strong taste. Available in varying degrees of intensity, so use according to your taste.

FLOUR
cake lower in protein than plain (all-purpose) flour so it produces a finer, more tender crumb in baking.
plain (all-purpose) unbleached wheat flour; the best for baking: has a lower protein (gluten) content than bread flour, which produces soft-textured baked products.
rice very fine, almost powdery, gluten-free flour; made from ground white rice. Used in baking, as a thickener and in some Asian noodles and desserts.
self-raising all-purpose flour with baking powder and salt added; make at home in the proportion of 1 cup flour to 2 teaspoons baking powder.

GELATINE we use dried (powdered) gelatine; it's also available in sheet form known as leaf gelatine: 3 teaspoons of dried gelatine (8g or one sachet) is about the same as four gelatine leaves. The two types are interchangable but leaf gelatine gives a much clearer mixture than dried gelatine.

GINGER
fresh also called green or root ginger; thick gnarled root of a tropical plant.
glacé fresh ginger root preserved in sugar syrup; crystallised ginger (sweetened with cane sugar) can be substituted if rinsed with warm water and dried before using.
ground also called powdered ginger; used as a flavouring in baking but cannot be substituted for fresh ginger.

GREASING/OILING PANS use butter (for sweet baking), oil or cooking-oil spray (for savoury baking) to grease baking pans. Use paper towel or a pastry brush to spread the oil or butter over the pan.

HARISSA a Moroccan paste made from dried chillies, cumin, garlic, oil and caraway seeds. Available from Middle Eastern food shops and supermarkets.

HAZELNUTS also called filberts; plump, grape-sized, rich, sweet nut having a brown skin that is removed by rubbing heated nuts together vigorously in a tea-towel.
ground made by grinding hazelnuts to a coarse flour texture; for use in baking or as a thickening agent.

KAFFIR LIME LEAVES also called bai magrood, sold fresh, dried or frozen; looks like two glossy dark green leaves joined end to end, forming a rounded hourglass shape. A strip of fresh lime peel may be substituted for each kaffir lime leaf.

KUMARA (ORANGE SWEET POTATO) Polynesian name of an orange-fleshed sweet potato often confused with yam.

LEEKS a member of the onion family, the leek resembles a green onion but is much larger and more subtle in flavour. Tender baby or pencil leeks can be eaten whole with minimal cooking but adult leeks are usually trimmed of most of the green tops then chopped and cooked.

LEMON GRASS also called takrai, serai or serah. A tall, clumping, lemon-smelling and tasting, sharp-edged aromatic tropical grass; the white lower part of the stem is used, finely chopped. Can be found fresh, dried, powdered and frozen, in supermarkets, greengrocers and Asian food shops.

MAPLE SYRUP distilled from the sap of sugar maple trees found only in Canada and the USA. Maple-flavoured syrup or pancake syrup is not an adequate substitute for the real thing.

MUSLIN inexpensive, undyed, loosely woven cotton fabric used in cooking to strain stocks and sauces.

MUSTARD
dijon pale brown, distinctively flavoured, mild-tasting french mustard.

wholegrain also known as seeded mustard. A french-style coarse-grain mustard made from crushed mustard seeds and dijon-style french mustard.

OIL

cooking spray we use a cooking spray made from canola oil.

olive made from ripened olives. Extra virgin and virgin are the first and second press, respectively, of the olives and are therefore considered the best; 'extra light' or 'light' refers to taste not fat levels.

peanut pressed from ground peanuts; most commonly used oil in Asian cooking because of its high smoke point (capacity to handle high heat without burning).

sesame made from roasted, crushed, white sesame seeds; used as a flavouring rather than a cooking medium.

vegetable sourced from plants rather than animal fats.

ONIONS

brown and white interchangeable although white onions have a more pungent flesh.

green (scallions) also called, incorrectly, shallot; an immature onion picked before the bulb has formed, has a long green stalk.

red also known as spanish, red spanish or bermuda onion; a sweet-flavoured, large, purple-red onion.

shallots also called french or golden shallots or eschalots; small and brown-skinned.

ORANGE BLOSSOM WATER

concentrated flavouring from orange blossoms.

PACKAGED BREADCRUMBS prepared fine-textured but crunchy white breadcrumbs; good for coating foods that are to be fried.

PAPRIKA ground, dried, sweet red capsicum (bell pepper); there are many grades and types available, including sweet, hot, mild and smoked.

PARSNIP has a nutty sweetness; can be substituted for potatoes. Available all year but the cold develops their sweet/savoury flavour in winter.

PEPITAS (PUMPKIN SEEDS) the pale green kernels of dried pumpkin seeds; available plain or salted.

PINE NUTS not a nut at all but a small, cream-coloured kernel from pine cones. They are best toasted first to bring out the flavour.

PLUM SAUCE a thick, sweet and sour dipping sauce made from plums, vinegar, sugar, chillies and spices.

POLENTA also known as cornmeal; a ground, flour-like cereal made of dried corn (maize). Also the name of the dish made from it.

POMEGRANATE dark-red, leathery-skinned fruit about the size of an orange filled with hundreds of seeds, each wrapped in an edible lucent-crimson pulp with a unique tangy sweet-sour flavour.

POMEGRANATE MOLASSES not to be confused with pomegranate syrup or grenadine; pomegranate molasses is thicker, browner, and more concentrated in flavour — tart and sharp, slightly sweet and fruity. Buy from Middle Eastern food stores or specialty food shops.

PROSCIUTTO an unsmoked Italian ham; salted, air-cured and aged, it is usually eaten uncooked.

RADICCHIO a red-leafed Italian chicory with a refreshing bitter taste that's eaten raw and grilled. Comes in varieties named after their places of origin, such as round-headed Verona or long-headed Treviso.

RICE

basmati a white, fragrant long-grained rice; the grains fluff up when cooked. Wash grains several times before cooking.

jasmine a long-grain white rice recognised as having a perfumed aromatic quality; moist in texture, it clings together after cooking. Can be substituted for basmati rice.

ROASTING/TOASTING nuts and dried coconut can be roasted in the oven to restore their fresh flavour and release their aromatic essential oils. Spread evenly onto an oven tray then roast in a moderate oven for about 5 minutes. Pine nuts, sesame seeds and desiccated coconut toast more evenly if stirred over low heat in a heavy-based frying pan.

ROCKET (ARUGULA) also called rugula and rucola; peppery green leaf eaten raw in salads or used in cooking. Baby rocket leaves are smaller and less peppery.

SOY SAUCE also called sieu; made from fermented soybeans. Several variations are available in supermarkets and Asian food stores; we use japanese soy sauce unless indicated otherwise.

SPINACH also called english spinach and, incorrectly, silver beet. Baby spinach leaves are best eaten raw in salads or cooked until barely wilted.

STAR ANISE dried star-shaped pod with an astringent aniseed flavour; used to flavour stocks and marinades. Available whole and ground, it is an essential ingredient in chinese five-spice.

SUGAR
brown a very soft, finely granulated sugar that has retained molasses for its colour and flavour.
caster (superfine) finely granulated table sugar; dissolves easily.
demerara small-grained golden-coloured crystal sugar.
icing (confectioners') also called powdered sugar; pulverised granulated sugar crushed together with a small amount of cornflour.
palm also called nam tan pip, jaggery, jawa or gula melaka; made from the sap of the sugar palm tree. Light brown to black in colour and usually sold in rock-hard cakes; use brown sugar instead.
pure icing (confectioners') also known as powdered sugar.
raw natural brown granulated sugar.

SUGAR SNAP PEAS also called honey snap peas; fresh small pea which can be eaten, whole, pod and all, similarly to snow peas.

SUMAC a purple-red, astringent ground spice; adds a tart, lemony flavour to dips and dressings. Can be found in Middle Eastern food stores.

TAMARIND the tamarind tree produces clusters of hairy brown pods, each of which is filled with seeds and a viscous pulp, that are dried and pressed into blocks of tamarind found in Asian food shops. Gives a sweet-sour, slightly astringent taste to marinades, pastes, sauces and dressings.

TAMARIND CONCENTRATE the distillation of tamarind pulp into a condensed, compacted paste. Thick and purple-black, it requires no soaking. Found in Asian food stores.

TOMATOES
canned whole peeled tomatoes in natural juices; available crushed, chopped or diced. Use undrained.
cherry also called tiny tim or tom thumb tomatoes; small and round.
grape small, long oval-shaped.
medley mixed baby tomatoes sold in prepacked punnets. Contains varieties such as grape, cherry, roma and kumato.
paste triple-concentrated tomato puree used to flavour soups, stews and sauces.
roma (egg) also called plum; smallish, oval-shaped tomatoes.
truss small vine-ripened tomatoes with vine still attached.

VANILLA
bean dried, long, thin pod from a tropical golden orchid; the minuscule black seeds inside the bean impart a luscious flavour in baking and desserts.
extract obtained from pulping and infusing vanilla beans in a mixture of alcohol and water.

paste made from vanilla beans and contains real vanilla bean seeds. It is concentrated: 1 teaspoon replaces a whole vanilla bean. Found in the baking section of most supermarkets.

VIETNAMESE MINT not a mint but a pungent and peppery narrow-leafed member of the buckwheat family.

VINEGAR
balsamic originally from Modena, Italy, there are now many balsamic vinegars on the market ranging in quality depending on how, and how long, they have been aged.
red wine based on a blend of fermented red wines.
tarragon white wine vinegar infused with fresh tarragon.

WATERCRESS one of the cress family, a large group of peppery greens. Highly perishable so it should be used as soon as possible after purchase.

WITLOF (BELGIAN ENDIVE) related to and confused with chicory. A versatile vegetable, it can be cooked or eaten raw. Grown in darkness like white asparagus to prevent it becoming green; looks somewhat like a tightly furled, cream to very light-green cigar.

YOGHURT, GREEK-STYLE plain yoghurt strained in a (traditionally muslin) cloth to remove the whey and to give it a creamy consistency.

ZUCCHINI also called courgette; small, pale- or dark-green or yellow vegetable of the squash family. Harvested when young, its edible flowers can be filled and deep-fried.

CONVERSION CHART

MEASURES

One Australian metric measuring cup holds approximately 250ml; one Australian metric tablespoon holds 20ml; one Australian metric teaspoon holds 5ml. The difference between one country's measuring cups and another's is within a two- or three-teaspoon variance, and will not affect your cooking results. North America, New Zealand and the United Kingdom use a 15ml tablespoon.

All cup and spoon measurements are level. The most accurate way of measuring dry ingredients is to weigh them. When measuring liquids, use a clear glass or plastic jug with the metric markings.

The imperial measurements used in these recipes are approximate only. Measurements for cake pans are approximate only. Using same-shaped cake pans of a similar size should not affect the outcome of your baking. We measure the inside top of the cake pan to determine sizes.

We use large eggs with an average weight of 60g.

DRY MEASURES

metric	imperial
15g	½oz
30g	1oz
60g	2oz
90g	3oz
125g	4oz (¼lb)
155g	5oz
185g	6oz
220g	7oz
250g	8oz (½lb)
280g	9oz
315g	10oz
345g	11oz
375g	12oz (¾lb)
410g	13oz
440g	14oz
470g	15oz
500g	16oz (1lb)
750g	24oz (1½lb)
1kg	32oz (2lb)

LIQUID MEASURES

metric	imperial
30ml	1 fluid oz
60ml	2 fluid oz
100ml	3 fluid oz
125ml	4 fluid oz
150ml	5 fluid oz
190ml	6 fluid oz
250ml	8 fluid oz
300ml	10 fluid oz
500ml	16 fluid oz
600ml	20 fluid oz
1000ml (1 litre)	1¾ pints

LENGTH MEASURES

metric	imperial
3mm	⅛in
6mm	¼in
1cm	½in
2cm	¾in
2.5cm	1in
5cm	2in
6cm	2½in
8cm	3in
10cm	4in
13cm	5in
15cm	6in
18cm	7in
20cm	8in
22cm	9in
25cm	10in
28cm	11in
30cm	12in (1ft)

OVEN TEMPERATURES

The oven temperatures in this book are for conventional ovens; if you have a fan-forced oven, decrease the temperature by 10-20 degrees.

	°C (Celsius)	°F (Fahrenheit)
Very slow	120	250
Slow	150	300
Moderately slow	160	325
Moderate	180	350
Moderately hot	200	400
Hot	220	425
Very hot	240	475

INDEX

A

anchovy butter 101
artichoke and asparagus fritters
    with olive relish 31
asian inspired menu 179
asparagus
    artichoke and asparagus fritters
        with olive relish 31
    roasted, and smashed potatoes
        139

B

baked ricotta with char-grilled
    vegetables 44
baklava, pistachio, walnut and
    chocolate 158
bao 77
    spiced tofu 77
beef
    barbecued steaks with corn salad
        101
    chipotle beef tostaditas 28
    fillet with garlic cream sauce 70
    steak with cashew nam jim and
        asian greens 69
    warm beef salad with chimichurri
        58
beetroot
    baby beetroot, lentil and watercress
        salad 132
    candied 169
    flourless chocolate beetroot cake
        169
    warm beetroot and heirloom carrot
        salad 123

berry and tamarillo croissant pudding
    cake 161
bruschetta
    haloumi and avocado 20
    roast pumpkin and fetta 32

C

cake
    berry and tamarillo croissant
        pudding cake 161
    flourless chocolate beetroot 169
    lime and passionfruit frozen
        yoghurt 146
    pistachio and lemon curd 162
    poached pear, mascarpone and
        dessert wine cake 173
    ricotta cakes with honey and
        roasted peaches 157
capsicum
    chicken and capsicum pies 86
carrot
    warm beetroot and heirloom carrot
        salad 123
cashew nam jim 69
casual lunch for girlfriends menu 178
celeriac and potato gratin 73
char-grilled quail with cauliflower
    salad 57
cherry blueberry compote 165
chicken
    chicken and capsicum pies 86
    fried buttermilk and mustard
        chicken wings 27
    lime leaf chicken 61
    paprika chicken with chilli sauce
        98

roast with broad beans and lemon
    65
chimichanga, shredded pork 19
chimichurri 58
    lamb cutlets 35
chinese roast duck with green onion
    pancakes 78
chipotle beef tostaditas 28
chocolate
    chocolate cherry berry pavlova 165
    flourless chocolate beetroot cake
        169
    sauce 166
chorizo
    chorizo, chickpea and pumpkin
        salad 105
    chorizo and potato fritters 11
cocktail party for a crowd menu 178
coconut
    coconut and prawn fritters with
        asian salad 93
    coconut panna cotta with mango
        and wafers 149
    rice 81
    wafers 149
coffee cream 166
comfort food menu 181
corn, mexican style barbecued 116
crab, soft shell with green onion aïoli
    39
créme fraîche
    harissa 82
    sweetened 169
croquettes, paella 23
crostata, plum and ginger 154
crunchy mung bean and coriander
    salad 120

cucumber
  pineapple and cucumber salad 77
curry
  slow-cooked red pork 74
  sri lankan seafood 81

D

dipping sauce 93
dressing 110, 119, 123
  hummus 128
  orange 136
  pickled sultana 135
  sherry vinegar 105
  sumac 52
duck, chinese roast with green onion
  pancakes 78

E

eggs
  individual egg, spinach and
    tomato bread cases 40

F

family gathering menu 179
fattoush 140
fennel, pickled 15, 82
fish
  creamy prawn and fish pie 109
  scrolls with capsicum salsa 12
five-spice squid with lime mayonnaise
  43
flatbreads, seeded 94
fried buttermilk and mustard
  chicken wings 27
fried oysters with salsa 36

fritters
  artichoke and asparagus with
    olive relish 31
  chorizo and potato 11
  coconut and prawn with asian
    salad 93
fruit
  macerated 174
  salad, middle-eastern style 150

G

gai lan with oyster sauce 127
garlic cream sauce 70
grapes, pickled 90
green barley salad 131
green onion
  aïoli 39
  chinese roast duck with green
    onion pancakes 78

H

haloumi and avocado bruschetta 20
harissa créme fraîche 82
honey syrup 158
hummus dressing 128

I

individual egg, spinach and tomato
  bread cases 40

J

jerk fish tacos with slaw and avocado
  cream 85

L

labne 119
lamb
  barbecued leg with lemon thyme
    salsa verde 66
  chimichurri lamb cutlets 35
  sumac chilli lamb 106
  tamarind and lemon grass lamb
    ribs 89
  tomato braised lamb shanks with
    creamy polenta 62
lemon curd 162
lemon thyme salsa verde 66
lettuce wedges with creamy lemon
  dressing 115
lime
  candied 146
  lime and passionfruit frozen
    yoghurt cake 146
  lime leaf chicken 61

M

mangoes
  caramelised 149
  mango and macadamia tart 177
mash 109
mayonnaise, lime 43
menus
  asian inspired 179
  casual lunch for girlfriends 178
  cocktail party for a crowd 178
  comfort food 181
  family gathering 179
  summer by the pool 180
  sunday brunch 181
  vegetarian feast 180

middle-eastern salad cups 52
mocha meringue stack 166
mushroom sliders with harissa
    créme fraîche 82

N

nam jim, cashew 69

O

olive
    relish 31
    sage and olive sautéed potatoes
        124
orange, candied blood 153
oysters, fried with salsa 36

P

pad thai, prawn 51
paella croquettes 23
pancakes, ricotta and basil with
    roasted tomatoes 16
panettone custard pudding with
    macerated fruit 174
pangrattato 24
paprika chicken with chilli sauce
    98
pasta
    rigatoni with oven-roasted
        vegetables 102
pastry 154
pavlova, chocolate cherry berry 165
peach and nectarine tart 170
pears
    pear, sage and goat's cheese
        seeded flatbreads 94

poached pear, mascarpone and
    dessert wine cake 173
pickled sultana dressing 135
pies
    chicken and capsicum 86
    creamy prawn and fish 109
pineapple and cucumber salad 77
pistachios
    pistachio, walnut and chocolate
        baklava 158
    pistachio and lemon curd 162
pistou 48
plums
    plum and ginger crostata 154
    sauce 78
polenta, creamy 62
pork
    shredded pork chimichanga 19
    slow-cooked red pork curry 74
    slow-roasted pork belly with
        crushed kumara 90
potatoes
    celeriac and potato gratin 73
    chorizo and potato fritters 11
    mash 109
    roasted asparagus and smashed
        potatoes 139
    sage and olive sautéed 124
prawn
    creamy prawn and fish pie 109
    pad thai 51
primavera soup with pangrattato 24
prosciutto and pea tart 110
pumpkin
    roast pumpkin and fetta bruschetta
        32
    roast pumpkin and parsnip with
        hummus dressing 128

Q

quail, char-grilled with cauliflower
    salad 57

R

ratatouille soup with pistou 48
red salad 143
rice, coconut 81
ricotta
    baked with char-grilled vegetables
        44
    ricotta and basil pancakes with
        roasted tomatoes 16
    ricotta cakes with honey and
        roasted peaches 157
rigatoni with oven-roasted
    vegetables 102

S

sage and olive sautéed potatoes 124
salad
    baby beetroot, lentil and watercress
        132
    chorizo, chickpea and pumpkin
        105
    crunchy mung bean and coriander
        120
    fattoush 140
    green barley salad 131
    middle-eastern salad cups 52
    pineapple and cucumber 77
    red 143
    supergreens with polenta croûtons
        135

tomato with labne and seeds 119
warm beef salad with chimichurri 58
warm beetroot and heirloom carrot 123
witlof, fennel and zucchini with orange dressing 136
salsa
  criolla 97
  lemon thyme salsa verde 66
  salsa verde 44
salmon, barbecued with salsa criolla 97
sambal, tomato 81
sauces
  caramel 149
  chilli 98
  chocolate 166
  dipping 93
  garlic cream 70
  plum 78
seafood
  barbecued salmon with salsa criolla 97
  creamy prawn and fish pie 109
  fish scrolls with capsicum salsa 12
  five-spice squid with lime mayonnaise 43
  fried oysters with salsa 36
  prawn pad thai 51
  smoked ocean trout and pickled fennel buns 15
  soft shell crab with green onion aïoli 39
  sri lankan seafood curry 81
seeded flatbreads 94
shredded pork chimichanga 19

sliders, mushroom with harissa créme fraîche 82
smoked ocean trout and pickled fennel buns 15
soup
  primavera with pangrattato 24
  ratatouille soup with pistou 48
squid
  five-spice squid with lime mayonnaise 43
steak
  barbecued with corn salad 101
  steak with cashew nam jim and asian greens 69
sumac
  dressing 52
  sumac chilli lamb 106
summer by the pool menu 180
sunday brunch menu 181
syrup
  honey 158
  lime 177

tacos, jerk fish with slaw and avocado cream 85
tamarind and lemon grass lamb ribs 89
tangelo tart with candied blood oranges 153
tarts
  mango and macadamia 177
  peach and nectarine 170
  prosciutto and pea 110
  tangelo with candied blood oranges 153
  zucchini 47

tofu
  spiced tofu bao 77
tomato
  individual egg, spinach and tomato bread cases 40
  ricotta and basil pancakes with roasted tomatoes 16
  sambal 81
  tomato braised lamb shanks with creamy polenta 62
  tomato salad with labne and seeds 119
tostaditas, chipotle beef 28

veal, roast rack with celeriac and potato gratin 73
vegetarian feast menu 180

wafers, coconut 149
walnut and ginger paste 154
white bean purée 106
witlof, fennel and zucchini salad with orange dressing 136

Y

yoghurt
  labne 119
  lime and passionfruit frozen yoghurt cake 146

Z

zucchini tarts 47

PUBLISHED IN 2015 BY BAUER MEDIA BOOKS, SYDNEY.
BAUER MEDIA BOOKS IS A DIVISION OF BAUER MEDIA PTY LTD.

BAUER MEDIA BOOKS

Publisher Jo Runciman
Editorial & food director Pamela Clark
Director of sales, marketing & rights Brian Cearnes
Creative director Hieu Chi Nguyen
Art director Hannah Blackmore
Designer Jeannel Cunanan
Food editor Emma Braz
Editor & contributing writer Amy Bayliss
Senior business analyst Rebecca Varela
Operations manager David Scotto
Special sales manager Simone Aquilina

Published by Bauer Media Books, a division of
Bauer Media Pty Ltd, 54 Park St, Sydney;
GPO Box 4088, Sydney, NSW 2001.
phone (02) 9282 8618; fax (02) 9267 9438
www.awwcookbooks.com.au

Special feature & cover photography
Photographer James Moffat
Stylist Vivien Walsh
Food preparation Sarah Murphy
Cover (from top left) Red salad, page 143; Barbecued
lamb leg with lemon thyme salsa verde, page 66;
Chorizo and potato fritters, page 11.
Back cover Tangelo tart with candied blood oranges,
page 153.

Printed in China with 1010 Printing.

Australia Distributed by Network Services,
phone +61 2 9282 8777; fax +61 2 9264 3278;
networkweb@networkservicescompany.com.au
New Zealand Distributed by Bookreps NZ Ltd
Phone (64 9) 419 2635 Fax (64 9) 419 2634
susan@bookreps.co.nz
South Africa Distributed by PSD Promotions,
phone +27 11 392 6065/6/7; fax +27 11 392 6079/80;
orders@psdprom.co.za

Title: Shared plates/Pamela Clark.
ISBN: 978 174245 604 1 (paperback)
Subjects: Cooking.
Other Authors/Contributors: Clark, Pamela, editor.
Dewey Number: 641.5

To order books
phone 136 116 (within Australia) or
order online at www.awwcookbooks.com.au
Send recipe enquiries to:
recipeenquiries@bauer-media.com.au